THE
*A*rab–Israeli
CONFLICT

TONY REA
AND JOHN WRIGHT

Oxford University Press, Great Clarendon Street, Oxford OX2 6DP England

Oxford New York

Auckland Cape Town Dar es Salaam Hong Kong Karachi Kuala Lumpur Madrid Melbourne Mexico City Nairobi New Delhi Shanghai Taipei Toronto

With offices in

Argentina Austria Brazil Chile Czech Republic France Greece Guatemala Hungary Italy Japan South Korea Poland Portugal Singapore Switzerland Thailand Turkey Ukraine Vietnam

Oxford is a trade mark of Oxford University Press

© Oxford University Press 1997
First published 1997
ISBN 9780199171705

10

Printed in China

The authors would like to thank Peter Allott for his help in researching part of the text.

In memory of Harry Turner.

The publishers would like to thank the following for permission to reproduce photographs:
Associated Press: p 55 (bottom), 62 (top), 73 (bottom), 77 (left); Camera Press: p 30 (bottom), 37, 43, 44, 47 (bottom), 62 (bottom), 77 (middle); Camera Press/Thierry Charlier: p 68 (bottom); Camera Press/IPPA: p 39; Camera Press/Claes Lufgren: p 50 (bottom); Camera Press/Christine Osbourne: pp 24 (top left), 65; Camera Press/David Rusinger: p 57 (top); Corbis/Bettmann: p 21; Corbis/Bettmann/UPI: p 25; Corbis/Jim Hollander/Reuters: p 47 (top); Mary Evans Picture Librry: pp 5, 12 (left), 76 (left); Stanley Gibbons Ltd: pp 23, 24 (bottom right); Hulton Getty Images: pp 9, 12 (right), 15, 21, 27, 34, 35, 42, 45, 46, 52 (top); Dr Garda Karmi: p 77 (right both); Magnum Photos: p 76 (right); Popperfoto: pp 10, 14, 17, 19, 26, 30 (top), 40, 52 (bottom), 55 (top), 56, 57 (bottom), 63, 68 (top right), 74 (top); Popperfoto/UPI: p 48; Popperfoto/Jack Dabbaghian: p 61; Popperfoto/Jack Dabbaghian/UPI: p 59 (bottom); Popperfoto/Nayef Hashlamoun/Reuters: pp 73 (top), 75; Popperfoto/Jim Hollander/Reuters: p 72; Popperfoto/Yoav Lemmer: p 4; Popperfoto/Havakuk Levinson/Reuters: p 71; Topham/Associated Press: p 41, 50 (top); Topham Picturepoint: p 22, 68 (top left), 70; Centre for the Study of Cartoons and Caricature, University of Kent, Canterbury/Steve Bell/The Guardian 27.9.96: p 74 (bottom); Centre for the Study of Cartoons and Caricature, University of Kent, Canterbury/Michael Cummings/Daily Express 23.11.56: p 66; Centre for the Study of Cartoons and Caricature, University of Kent, Canterbury/Emmwood(John Musgrave-Wood)/Daily Mail 30.10.73: p 54; Centre for the Study of Cartoons and Caricature, University of Kent, Canterbury/Les Gibbard/The Guardian 18.11.77: p 58; Centre for the Study of Cartoons and Caricature, University of Kent, Canterbury/Ken Waite/The Sun 11.7.67: p 67.

The publishers have made every effort to trace the copyright holders of all photographs, but in some cases have been unable to do so. They would welcome any information which would enable them to rectify this.

Designed by Peter Tucker, Holbrook Design Oxford Ltd
Maps by Jeff Edwards
Illustrations and diagrams by Peter Tucker

Contents

Preface

This book has been written specifically for students studying GCSE History, and it covers all of the GCSE objectives. It is a comprehensive coverage of the Arab-Israeli Conflict up to the present day. This makes the book suitable for use either as a topic book for students following one of the Twentieth-Century World syllabuses, and doing a Depth, Outline or Coursework study on the Middle East; or as a Modern World Study for students taking an SHP syllabus.

A large number of primary and secondary sources are integrated with the detailed and strongly narrative text. Maps, diagrams and photographs both enliven the text and enhance the students' understanding of it. The book is further enhanced with biographies of key individuals and 'feature' spreads, which enable students to reflect upon the text and consolidate their learning. These lively spreads encourage students to re-read and process the text, as well as presenting them with challenging and structured tasks. As they focus upon evidence skills as well as historical concepts, many of these spreads can be used as coursework assignments for GCSE, or as 'dry run' assignments with which to prepare students.

At the back of the book are two blank pages. These are 'update pages' which, in future editions, will be filled with post 1997 developments in the conflict. In this edition, however, teachers might like to encourage their students to select newspaper clippings of recent developments which can then be glued into the update pages or kept in a separate file.

1 *Background to the conflict*

A

> **Israel abused Human Rights**
>
> The decision by the Israeli government to build a Jewish neighbourhood in East Jerusalem is contrary to international law and 'a very severe concern', the United Nations' investigator on human rights in the Palestinian territories said yesterday. Israel had confiscated Arab owned land, used live ammunition against Palestinian demonstrators, and closed borders preventing Palestinians from going to work in Israel. This is all against international law.

An extract from *The Guardian*, 13 March 1997.

Source A contains an example of the problems which make up the Arab-Israeli conflict. A dispute between the Israelis (Jews) and the Palestinians (Arabs), with the United Nations trying to act as mediator. The decision in 1997 to build Jewish homes in East Jerusalem seemed to increase tension in the Middle East; and the shooting incident on the Jordanian-Israeli border in March 1997 (Source B) showed that the peace process had not created a lasting settlement.

The issues at stake in this area are not new ones, they go back thousands of years. The Jews and the Arabs have lived in the area of Palestine for more than three thousand years. Each has stated that its claim to own Palestine is greater than its opponents'. The conflict that has developed has emerged out of history, religion, and the unique geographical position of Palestine.

The Jews and Palestine

The Jews were driven out of Palestine by the Romans after two revolts in AD 70 and AD 135. Jews were forbidden to live in Palestine and had to settle wherever they could. Often they were persecuted and were forced to wander from country to country. Hatred of the Jews (anti-Semitism) stemmed from a variety of reasons. They were seen as 'Christ killers', as an elite group which considered itself to be the 'Chosen People', and as wicked money lenders. By the end of the nineteenth century, anti-Semitism was commonplace in Europe, for example, there were organised attacks on Jews in Russia (called 'pogroms'). It has been estimated that about three million Jews fled Eastern Europe in the thirty years before 1914 in order to escape persecution.

It was at this time that a movement developed, called Zionism, which set out to establish a Jewish national home. The idea of a national home was put forward by Theodor Herzl.

B

Israeli schoolgirls mourn the death of 7 of their friends in March 1997. A Jordanian soldier opened fire on an Israeli school party who were visiting a nature reserve on the Jordanian border with Israel. This incident happened on the same day (13 March 1997) that Source A was published.

Theodor Herzl

'Let us Jews be given sovereignty over part of the world big enough to satisfy the rightful needs of a nation.'

▼ Born 1860
▼ Jewish writer and journalist
▼ Founder of Zionism
▼ Regarded as one of the greatest influences in the movement that led to the creation of the state of Israel
▼ Died 1904

Herzl was born in Hungary where he became a well-known playwright. He worked in France where he witnessed the violent anti-Semitism that broke out in 1894 as a result of the court-martial of a Jewish army officer. Until then, Herzl had believed that a gradual joining together of the Jews with the Christians of Europe was the best solution to anti-Semitism, but in 1896 Herzl published *The Jewish State* which suggested the establishment of a Jewish homeland. Although this solution had already been suggested by other Jewish leaders, Herzl was the first to call for immediate action.

One year after writing *The Jewish State*, Herzl organised the first Zionist Congress in Basel, Switzerland. There were 206 delegates from 16 countries. The delegates issued the Basel Declaration, which presented as the main aim of Zionism 'to create for the Jewish people a homestead in Palestine secured by public law.'

In 1900, Herzl set up the Jewish Colonial Trust to provide funds for Jewish settlers to go to Palestine.

Herzl died in 1904, long before his dream of a Jewish homeland became a reality. In 1949 his remains were taken to a mountain west of Jerusalem that was named Mount Herzl.

If I had to sum up what happened at the Congress of Basel, I would say that I founded the Jewish state. This would provoke universal laughter today. But perhaps in twenty years and certainly in fifty, it will be there for all the world to see.

Theodor Herzl commenting in his diary about the Basel Congress, 1897.

By 1914, the Jewish population in Palestine was about 85,000. The Arab population at that time was about 650,000.

The Arabs and Palestine

In the early Middle Ages, the Arabs controlled a huge empire covering the Middle East, North Africa, and South Western Europe. Like most empires, it gradually fell into decline. The Arabs were, themselves, eventually absorbed into the Turkish Empire by the sixteenth century. Many Arabs wanted independence from the Turks, and, in 1913, the First Arab National Congress was held. In the following year, the Arab Nationalist Manifesto was published and it put forward the main ideas of those Arabs who wanted independence.

O ye Arabs!... You all dwell in one land, you speak in one language, so be also one nation and one land. Do not become divided amongst yourselves.

Extracts from the Arab Nationalist Manifesto, 1913.

By 1914 there were two rival groups in Palestine and each was beginning to view the territory as a homeland. There were even fights between the two groups where the Jews had established their own farming settlements (kibbutzim) in areas where many Arabs were also living.

Now that you have read about the background to the conflict, use the following section to help you to understand the key issue of the conflict, 'whose land is it anyway?'.

Whose land is it anyway?

So, this is the question at the root of the Arab-Israeli conflict. As you would expect, the answer is far from easy. Arabs and Jews each have a claim to the land which we now call Israel. To understand their claims, let us consider what some Arabs and Jews have written about their claims to this land.

'This is our homeland. Our ancestors lived here in ancient times.'

'This is our homeland. God promised it to us in ancient times.'

The land of Israel was the birth place of the Israeli people. Here their identity was made. Here they gained independence and created a culture. Here they wrote and gave the Bible to the world.

Driven out of Palestine, the Jewish people remained faithful. They never stopped praying and hoping for their return to their homeland and the restoration of their freedom. The United Nations recognition of the right of the Jewish people to have an independent homeland can not be cancelled. It is the right of the Jewish people to be a nation, like other nations, in its own country.

Adapted from the Israeli Declaration of Independence, 1948.

B

The problem is the story of people who lived peacefully in their own homes for generations. Then along came total strangers from across the sea who turned the people out of their country and occupied their homes. Some of these strangers may have been the victims of European terror, but most are pawns in a political movement. The Arab case is based on the principle that the only people who can claim ownership of their country are those who are born there and have had long and continued possession. It is the same case as that which gives the British the right to Britain.

Adapted from a modern Arab writer describing the problem from an Arab point of view.

C

'Next year, in Jerusalem!'

A traditional farewell of Jews who do not live in Israel.

D

We have unified Jerusalem, the divided capital of Israel. We have returned to the Holiest of our Holy places, never to part from it again.

The Israeli Defence Minister, Moshe Dayan, speaking in 1967 when Israeli soldiers had just captured East Jerusalem.

E

Our Palestinian consciousness was increased and took on a new dimension. It was kept alive by two things: the preservation of our memory of Palestine and the education we received. We continued to refuse houses and compensation offered by the UN to settle us in our host countries. We wanted nothing short of our return to our homeland.

And from Syria, Lebanon, and Jordan we would see a few miles, a few yards, across the borders a land where we had been born. A land where we had lived and where we felt the earth. 'This is my land' we would shout, or cry, or sing, or plead, or reason.

Written by the Palestinian Arab writer Fawaz Turki, who grew up in one of the refugee camps outside Israel.

1 What does the author of Source B mean by 'the victims of European terror'?
2 The author of Source B says 'the only people who can claim ownership of their country are those who are born there and have had long and continued possession'. Which group, the Arabs or the Jews, have been born in Israel and have had long and continued possession of the land?
3 In what ways do Sources C and D help you understand the importance of Jerusalem to the Jews?
4 After reading this chapter and all of these sources, can you decide who has the stronger claim to Palestine, the Arabs or the Jews?

2 The establishment of a Jewish homeland and state, 1914–48

The impact of the First World War

The First World War was a turning point for the Jews and the Arabs. During the war, the interests of Turkey and Britain determined the fate of the people of Palestine. Turkey declared war on Britain in 1914, and this immediately gave rise to fears that the security of Britain's empire in the Indian sub-continent would be threatened. Britain also feared that its vital oil supplies from Persia would be cut off.

To counter this Turkish threat, Britain decided to enlist the help of the Arabs. This was a change in policy, because in the past Britain and Turkey had been allies against the threat of Russia. To secure the help of the Arabs, Britain promised to support them in their struggle for independence from Turkey.

Having made one promise to the Arabs, Britain then made an open statement supporting the establishment of a Jewish homeland in Palestine. Britain thought that Jews in the USA would put pressure on their government to enter the war on Britain's side, and that Jews in Russia would pressure their government to remain in the war.

Britain and the promise to the Arabs

The recognised leader of the Arab world was Sherif Hussein of Mecca. Negotiations between Britain and the Sherif were led by Sir Henry McMahon, the British High Commissioner in Egypt. Hussein's demands were set out in a letter to McMahon in July 1915.

Firstly, Britain should acknowledge the independence of the Arab countries, bounded on the north by Mersin and Adana up to the 37th degree of latitude, on which degree are Birejik, Urfa, Mardin... Amadia, up to the border of Persia; on the east by the borders of Persia up to the Gulf of Basra; on the south by the Indian Ocean, with the exception of the position of Aden to remain as it is; on the west by the Red Sea up to Mersin.

From a letter by Sherif Hussein to McMahon, 1915.

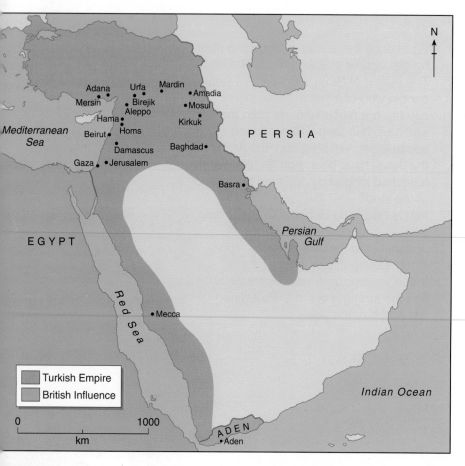

The area of the Middle East refered to in the letters between Sir Henry McMahon and Sherif Hussein, 1915

Later in 1915, McMahon responded by letter to Hussein's demands.

Subject to modifications, Great Britain is prepared to recognise and support the independence of the Arabs in all regions within the limits demanded by the Sherif of Mecca... When the situation allows, Great Britain will give to the Arabs her advice and will assist them to establish what may appear to be the most suitable forms of government in those various territories. I am convinced that this declaration assures you beyond all possible doubt of the sympathy of Great Britain towards the aspirations of her friends the Arabs and will result in a firm and lasting alliance, the immediate result of which will be the expulsion of the Turks.

From McMahon's letter to Sherif Hussein, 1915.

The modifications that McMahon suggested were outlined in the same letter.

Areas of Syria lying to the west of the districts of Damascus, Homs, Hama and Aleppo, cannot be said to be purely Arab and should be excluded from Hussein's demands.

From McMahon's letter to Sherif Hussein, 1915.

Two parts of McMahon's letter to Hussein stored up problems for the future. One was in the interpretation of the modification proposed by McMahon, the other was in the phrase 'when the situation allows'. In 1937, McMahon wrote to *The Times*.

I feel it is my duty to state that it was not intended by me in giving this pledge to Hussein to include Palestine in the area in which Arab independence was promised.

An extract from McMahon's letter to *The Times*, 1937.

Arab guerrillas in the Jordanian desert in July 1917

The Arabs accepted the British promises and raised an army to fight the Turks. The army was led by Prince Faisal, who was assisted by Colonel T E Lawrence (who gained the nickname 'Lawrence of Arabia' as a result of his exploits in the Middle East campaigns). By 1918, the Arab and British forces had defeated the Turks and it seemed that independence would be granted as soon as the war between Britain and Germany ended. However, the British had not played completely fair with the Arabs. In 1916, a secret agreement had been made with France which would partition the Turkish Empire. The Sykes-Picot Agreement seemed to show that Britain and France were still interested in grabbing as much land as possible. Details of the agreement were published by the Russians and the plans were quickly dropped. The Arabs were angry at the way Britain had behaved, but their concern grew even more when the Balfour Declaration was announced.

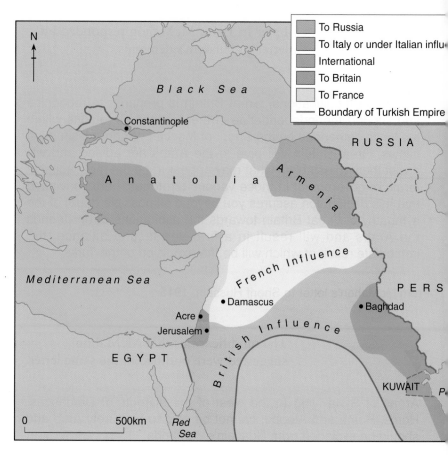

The division of the Turkish Empire proposed in the Sykes-Picot Agreement, 1916

Britain and the promise to the Jews

The Balfour Declaration was made on 2 November 1917 in a letter from the British Foreign Secretary, Arthur Balfour, to Lord Rothschild, an influential member of the Jewish community.

E

I have much pleasure in conveying to you, on behalf of His Majesty's Government, the following declaration of sympathy with Jewish Zionist aspirations which has been submitted to, and approved by, the Cabinet.
  'His Majesty's Government view with favour the establishment in Palestine of a national home for the Jewish people... it being clearly understood that nothing shall be done which may prejudice the civil and religious rights of existing non-Jewish communities in Palestine.'

Lord Balfour in Tel Aviv with Dr Chaim Weizman, one of the main Zionist leaders

Extracts from the Balfour Declaration, 1917.

There are different interpretations of Britain's willingness to issue the Balfour Declaration. Was it to involve the USA in the war, or to keep Russia in the war (both countries had large Jewish populations); or was it to secure the friendship of any new government near the Suez Canal?

When the First World War ended, both the Arabs and the Jews experienced disappointment – independence was not granted to either side. Instead, Palestine became a 'mandated territory' governed by Britain, despite the idea of self-determination put forward by President Wilson of the USA. Independence would only be granted when Britain thought Palestine was ready for self-government.

The terms of the mandate will embody the substance of the Declaration of 1917. Arabs will not be removed from their land nor required to leave the country. There is no question of majority being subjected to the rule of minority.

Lord Curzon, British Foreign Secretary, August 1919.

 The actual division of the Turkish Empire into League of Nations mandates

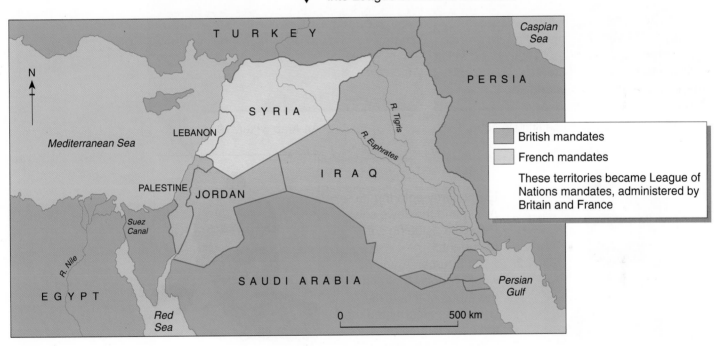

British mandates

French mandates

These territories became League of Nations mandates, administered by Britain and France

In Palestine we do not propose to go through the form of consulting the wishes of the present inhabitants of the country... Zionism, be it right or wrong, good or bad, is rooted in age long traditions of far greater meaning than the desires and prejudices of the 700,000 Arabs who now inhabit that ancient land.

From a memo written by Arthur Balfour at the Versailles Peace Conference 1919.

1 Describe the promises made to the Arabs by the British Government.
2 What did the Balfour Declaration promise the Jews?
3 Why did Britain make promises to both the Arabs and the Jews?
4 In what ways were both the Arabs and Jews disappointed at the end of the First World War?

Like everything in history, the Arab-Israeli conflict is made up of long term and short term causes. Among the long term causes are the expulsion of the Jews from Palestine by the Romans, the conversion of the Arabs to Islam, and the Turkish occupation of Palestine which lasted until 1918. During this long period, from AD70 to 1918, there were a number of changes in Palestine, which you can see in the time line at the foot of the page, but there was also a great deal of continuity. The changes which happened were important, but they did not happen quickly. However, by 1918, both the Arabs and the Jews believed that they had the right to live and rule themselves in their own land. Palestine.

The settlement of Jews in Palestine will not be a sudden one. It will be gradual, continuous and will take many years. The poorest will go first to farm the soil. They will also build roads, bridges and railways. They will control the rivers and build their own houses. Their work will bring trade, trade will create markets and markets will attract new settlers.

Theodor Herzl speaking in 1896.

Arise, O you Arabs. Take out the sword from the scabbard. Do not let an oppressive tyrant who only looks down on you remain in your country. Clean your country of those who show their hatred to you, to your race and to your language.

An Arab writer, 1914.

1 Explain why both the Arabs and the Jews saw Palestine as being so important.
2 From Sources A and B, would you say that either the Arabs or the Jews seem less determined than the other to gain an independent homeland?

600–700 Most Arabs were converted to the Muslim religion.

| 0 | 100 | 200 | 300 | 400 | 500 | 600 | 700 | 800 | 900 |

70 First Jewish revolt against the Romans.

135 Second revolt and expulsion of Jews from Palestine. The Jews begin to settle in Europe.

Arab-Israeli conflict?

It was during the years of the First World War, 1914-1918, that events concerning Palestine began to quicken up. This period has been described as a turning point in the Arab-Israeli conflict. A turning point means a great change in the direction of events.

The War brought Britain and Turkey into conflict with each other in the Middle East and Palestine. Britain needed the help of both the Arabs living in the Middle East and of the USA. For this reason, Britain made two key promises, which you have already seen.

The McMahon promise to Sherif Hussein

Page 9

The Balfour Declaration

Page 10

Then, after the war, the victorious powers took Turkey's empire away. Britain gained control of Palestine when it was given a Mandate to govern there by the League of Nations.

The League of Nations Mandate

Page 14

3 In what ways did the Balfour Declaration and the League of Nations Mandate encourage Jews to go to Palestine?

4 How would each of these proclamations; the Balfour Declaration, the McMahon Promise, and the League of Nations Mandate affect both the Arabs and the Jews?

5 All three sources (the Balfour Declaration, the McMahon Promise, and the League of Nations Mandate) are official documents. What are the advantages and disadvantages of official documents for historians?

6 Find all of the evidence you can which is relevant to the question 'was the First World War a turning point in the Arab-Israeli conflict?' Arrange the evidence in two lists – yes and no.

7 Do you think the First World War was a turning point in the Arab-Israeli conflict? Did it make a great change in the situation for the better or for the worse? Did it bring about a great change in the direction of events? What do you think?

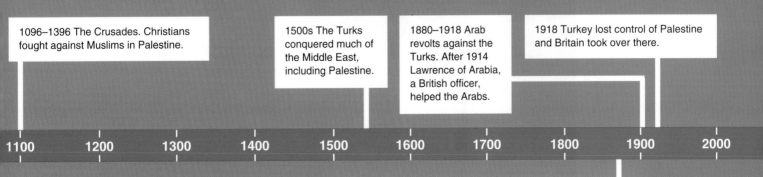

1096–1396 The Crusades. Christians fought against Muslims in Palestine.

1500s The Turks conquered much of the Middle East, including Palestine.

1880–1918 Arab revolts against the Turks. After 1914 Lawrence of Arabia, a British officer, helped the Arabs.

1918 Turkey lost control of Palestine and Britain took over there.

| 1100 | 1200 | 1300 | 1400 | 1500 | 1600 | 1700 | 1800 | 1900 | 2000 |

1880s Pogroms, anti Jewish riots, in Russia. Many Jews begin to move westward to Poland and Germany, as well as to the USA.

Palestine under the British mandate

The period between the two world wars in Palestine was one of unrest and violence. Both the Arab and Jewish communities fought each other, and, in the years 1936–39, the Arabs openly revolted against the British. Jewish hostility towards Britain began to flare in 1939, and extremists (such as the Stern Gang) attacked British targets that year and throughout the Second World War.

The first problem facing the British authorities after 1919 was the increasing Jewish immigration. The new settlers often bought land and would not employ Arab workers. The Arabs felt that the Jews were concentrating their settlements in specific places, and this was leading to areas which contained few Arabs. Tension grew between the two communities and, in May 1921, there were violent clashes at the port of Jaffa. (Jaffa was the main arrival point for Jewish immigrants.) The fighting left 200 Jews dead and 120 wounded. Britain temporarily stopped Jewish immigration but it was soon restarted. The Arabs became more convinced that they would not be granted independence following various statements from the League of Nations' Mandates Commission.

Britain shall be responsible for placing the country under such political, administrative and economic conditions as will secure the establishment of the Jewish national home and the development of self-governing institutions, and also for safeguarding the civil and religious rights of all the inhabitants of Palestine irrespective of race or religion.

League of Nations' Mandates Commission, 1922.

The Arabs felt that they had swapped one imperial power for another. Resentment between the two communities did not fade away and there were renewed outbreaks of rioting in 1929, when 133 Jews and 116 Arabs were killed. Britain considered restricting Jewish immigration, but pro-Jewish groups in Britain and the USA opposed such a suggestion and the government dropped it. However, the issue of immigration would not go away, and, after 1933, the number of Jewish immigrants rose more quickly following the persecution of Jews in Germany by the Nazis. For those escaping the tyranny of the Nazis, Palestine was not only a homeland but a sanctuary.

Jewish homes set alight by Arab rioters during the Jaffa riots of May 1921

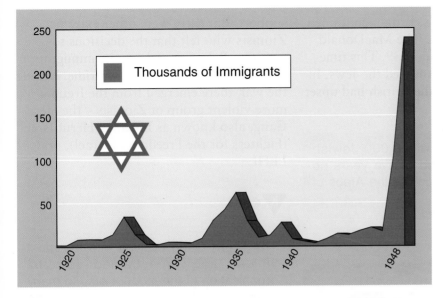

Legend: **Thousands of Immigrants**

(Chart axis values: 250, 200, 150, 100, 50)

(Years: 1920, 1925, 1930, 1935, 1940, 1948)

Jewish immigrants
into Palestine,
1918–1948

The years before the Second World War saw the situation worsen. In 1936, a serious Arab revolt broke out which lasted for three years and resulted in Britain having to send out large numbers of troops in order to keep control. In the first six months of the Arab revolt, 89 Jews were killed and more than 300 were injured. Britain set up a special police force called the Notrim which was to act as a militia to protect Jewish settlements. The Notrim soon became a legal cover for the Haganah (the Jewish Defence Force) and had several thousand members.

Official British figures for the death toll in 1938 were:

	Killed	Injured
Arab civilians	486	636
Arab rebels	1,138	196
Jews	292	649
British security forces	69	233

The Arab revolt did make Britain re-think its position, and, in 1937, the Peel Commission reported. It recommended that Palestine should be partitioned, with Arab and Jewish states separated by a British buffer zone.

There is no common ground between the Jews and the Arabs. They differ in religion and in language. Their cultural and social life, their ways of thought and conduct, are as incompatible as their national aspirations... Neither Arab nor Jew has any sense of service to a single State... The National Home cannot be half-national.

From the Peel Commission, 1937.

The Arabs continued their revolt and to their surprise and dismay found that the Haganah was being given help by the British. The methods used by the British to quell the revolt served to foster greater hatred among the Arabs – hostage taking, collective fines, destruction of houses suspected of harbouring Arabs involved in the revolt, hangings, and torture.

Arab prisoners are marched off to prison by British soldiers in 1938

Despite the upheavals, Britain continued to search for a solution. The MacDonald Report was published in 1939. This time the proposed solution angered the Jews. In a period of two years, the British had upset both sides in Palestine.

For each of the next five years a quota of 10,000 Jewish immigrants will be allowed... after the period of five years no further Jewish immigration will be permitted unless the Arabs of Palestine allow it.

From the Macdonald Report, 1939.

The cover of a Zionist publication in 1938. It shows Palestine as the promised land for Jews

When war broke out in September 1939, there were few Jews who did not support Britain in its fight against Germany. Even the Irgun Zvai Leumi, an extreme Zionist group, agreed that Britain should be given support. But there were other extreme Zionists who felt that the decisions to partition Palestine and restrict immigration should be opposed even in wartime. During the war, there emerged from the Irgun a more violent group of Zionists – the Stern Gang, also known as Lohamei Herut Israel (Fighters for the Freedom of Israel), or LEHI.

The Stern Gang evolved into the most violent and unrestrained terrorist organisation of the modern era. To many people the Stern Gang remains the example of terrorism – a tiny group of men without restraint, driven by dreams and fantasies, rebels beyond compromise, demented gunmen in pursuit of the impossible.

From *Terror out of Zion* by J B Bell, 1977.

As the war went on, the Stern Gang committed various acts of terrorism, and even attempted to assassinate the British High Commissioner in Palestine. In 1944, Menachem Begin, leader of Irgun, openly proclaimed the beginning of a Jewish revolt.

There is no longer any armistice between the Jewish people and the British Administration in Israel which hands our brothers over to Hitler. Our people are at war with Britain – a war to the end... Our demand is that there should be an immediate transfer of power in Israel to a provisional Jewish government. We shall fight, every Jew in the homeland will fight. There will be no retreat. Freedom or death.

Menachem Begin, 1944.

The activities of Irgun and the Stern Gang became increasingly serious during 1944 and 1945. Bridges and roads were destroyed and funds to finance the groups came from burglaries and bank and post office raids. Eventually, British soldiers were killed and there were high casualties among the local police force.

The British were forced to send more troops to maintain order, and, by 1946, there were almost 100,000 British soldiers in Palestine. The reactions of the British to the terrorists' activities were heavy handed but ineffective, and upset those Jews who thought that a peaceful compromise could be found.

In July 1946, the Irgun planted bombs in the King David Hotel in Jerusalem, where the British Military Headquarters in Palestine was based. The official casualty figures were 91 dead and 45 injured. The British found it difficult to arrest those responsible and resorted to mass interrogations.

During 1946, the British were also faced with an increasing number of illegal Jewish immigrants trying to settle in Palestine. Many of these people were survivors of the Nazi Holocaust and had experiences of concentration camps such as Auschwitz and Treblinka. Britain prevented their entry to Palestine and placed some in refugee camps in Cyprus. There were soon more than 10,000 people in such camps. When the ship *Exodus* arrived in Palestine in the summer of 1947, with 4,554 refugees, Britain refused entry to them all and returned them to their port of departure – Hamburg, Germany. Such action did not win Britain much support in the world.

The continued violence of the Jewish terrorist groups forced Britain to announce in February 1947 that the problem of Palestine was being referred to the newly created United Nations. The United Nations Special Committee on Palestine (the twenty-second committee to investigate the future of Palestine) decided that partition of the territory was the best solution, and, on 29 November 1947, voted for the creation of a Jewish state. For many Jews in Palestine there was great rejoicing. However, the following day, a group of Arabs opened fire on a bus outside Jerusalem and killed seven Jews.

The Jewish refugee ship, Theodor Herzl, arrives at the Port of Haifa in April 1947. The banner on the side reads 'The Germans destroyed our families and homes – don't you destroy our hopes'.

Turning Point: 1947

Why did the British leave Palestine?

Palestine had become a British Mandate in 1919 (see page 11) and for many years it was very important to the British. In 1947 Britain suddenly announced that it would leave Palestine, and hand over control of the area to the United Nations Organisation. Why did the British change their policy on Palestine?

First, the situation in Palestine had changed greatly during the 1930s.

The British were in an impossible position: if they allowed unrestricted immigration of Jews, Arab fears and violence would increase, but if they stopped or controlled immigration, the world would accuse them of inhumanity, of not caring for the Jews who were being persecuted by the Nazis in Germany.

In 1936 armed bands, led by local Arab leaders, began to attack Jewish settlements. Within a month over 20 Jews had been killed. By midsummer Palestine was caught up in a civil war which was to last for three years and cost hundreds of lives. The British decided to end the fighting by using soldiers and harsh punishments. They hanged several Arab mayors and destroyed houses suspected of containing Arab terrorists or weapons. The British also helped to organise the Jewish Defence force, called the Haganah?

From a British history book written in 1984.

A conflict has arisen between two national communities within the narrow bounds of one small country. About 1,000,000 Arabs are in strife with some 400,000 Jews.

Their national hopes are the greatest bar to peace. The First World War inspired all Arabs with the hope of reviving, in a free and united Arab world, the tradition of the Arab 'golden age'. The Jews are inspired by their historic past. They mean to show what the Jewish nation can achieve when restored to the land of its birth. National assimilation between Arabs and Jews seems to be ruled out.

From the British Peel Commission Report on Palestine, 1937. The report followed an inquiry into the problems in Palestine carried out by a Royal Commission which the British Government set up to get information.

It is proposed to set up within ten years an independent Palestine State, in which Arabs and Jews combine in government in such a way as to make sure that the essential interests of each community are safeguarded.

From the Macdonald Report, 1939.

1. What do the Royal Commissioners mean when they say in Source B 'national assimilation between Arabs and Jews seems to be ruled out'?
2. If the Commissioners felt that national assimilation between Arabs and Jews was ruled out, why do you think the White Paper (Source C) recommended 'an independent Palestine State, in which Arabs and Jews combine in government'?
3. Using Chapter 2 and Sources A, B, and C, make two lists. One list is of everything the British did to favour the Arabs. The second list is of everything the British did to favour the Jews.
4. Who seems to have benefited most from the action of the British – the Arabs or the Jews? Explain your answer.

By their methods, the British had managed to anger both the Arabs and the Jews. Jewish immigration continued, especially after the Second World War ended in 1945, and so did the violence. But now the violence became directed against the British. In 1946 Jewish fighters attacked the British Army Headquarters inside the King David Hotel in Jerusalem.

However, this pressure from within Palestine provides only some of the reasons for Britain's withdrawal from Palestine. 1945 had seen the election of a Labour government in Britain. This new government was committed to allowing more countries to rule themselves. In the years 1947 and 1948, as well as pulling out

of Palestine, Labour granted independence to India, Pakistan, Burma, and Ceylon.

Another factor was the state of the British economy and the cost of government plans for Britain. The economy was in ruin and debt. Labour also had great plans for social reforms such as the National Health Service and a welfare state. Staying on in Palestine was simply too expensive (see diagram below).

Finally, public opinion in Britain was sick of the violence and loss of life in Palestine, especially as British soldiers were being killed.

Once the British left, the Jewish State of Israel was proclaimed. Therefore, the course of events in the Arab-Israeli conflict seemed to change direction in 1947.

▲ The damaged King David Hotel in Jerusalem after the Jewish bomb attack

▼ Britain's financial position at the end of the Second World War

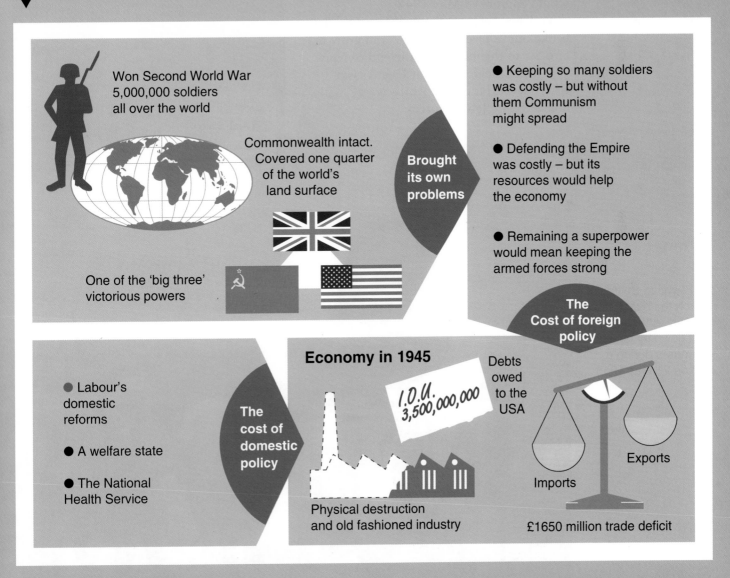

Won Second World War 5,000,000 soldiers all over the world

Commonwealth intact. Covered one quarter of the world's land surface

One of the 'big three' victorious powers

Brought its own problems

● Keeping so many soldiers was costly – but without them Communism might spread

● Defending the Empire was costly – but its resources would help the economy

● Remaining a superpower would mean keeping the armed forces strong

The Cost of foreign policy

● Labour's domestic reforms

● A welfare state

● The National Health Service

The cost of domestic policy

Economy in 1945

I.O.U. 3,500,000,000

Debts owed to the USA

Physical destruction and old fashioned industry

Imports

Exports

£1650 million trade deficit

3 The war years, 1948–1973

The United Nations' decision to partition Palestine meant that two states would be created – one Jewish and one Arab. Neither side could accept the idea of their homeland being divided and hostilities between the two soon broke out. The Palestinian Arabs rejected the idea of partition because they outnumbered the Jews and yet they were to be given less territory than the Jews. Many Jews could not accept that the partition meant that Jerusalem would not be included in their area. Britain announced that its mandate would end on 15 May 1948.

Violence between the Arabs and the Jews broke out in December 1947 and grew in ferocity in the months to the end of May. The worst incident was at Deir Yassin where several hundred Arabs were murdered by Jewish forces.

▶ The proposed UN partition plan for Palestine

Map legend:
- Jewish State
- Arab State
- International zone

Labels on map: SYRIA, Mediterrranean Sea, Jerusalem, PALESTINE, EGYPT, TRANSJORDAN, 0 — 100 km

▶ An Egyptian Spitfire lies on the beach near Tel Aviv, after being shot down by Israeli defenders during a raid on 21 May 1948

The War of 1948–1949

David Ben-Gurion

▶

David Ben-Gurion
pictured in 1946

- ▼ Born 1886
- ▼ Active Zionist
- ▼ Left Poland in 1906 to live in Palestine
- ▼ Israeli Prime Minister 1948-1953 and 1955-1963
- ▼ Died 1973

Ben-Gurion was dedicated to establishing a Jewish state in Israel and, by the age of 14, had established himself in the Zionist Youth League in Poland. In 1910 he gave up farming in Palestine to edit the Zionist workers newspaper, *Achdut*. Ben-Gurion welded together the Haganah and underground fighters into an army which defeated the invading Arabs in 1948, and, when the Republic of Israel was proclaimed, he became its first Prime Minister. Ben-Gurion led his country for a total of 15 years, promoting immigration, education, and the development of the desert lands into productive farms. He resigned from office in 1963, and, in 1970, left politics altogether in order to study and write. Ben-Gurion died on a Kibbutz in 1973.

In April 1948, the Jews captured the city of Haifa, which was designated part of the new Arab state in the UN partition plan. On the last day of the mandate, the Jews proclaimed the independence of the state of Israel. They then waited to be attacked by the neighbouring Arab countries. On 15 May, three Egyptian Spitfires attacked Tel Aviv airport. The Jews were unable to offer any defence. They had no anti-aircraft guns and no combat fighters. The outlook did not seem favourable.

Five Arab countries invaded Israel – Lebanon, Transjordan, Syria, Egypt, and Iraq. Many people expected the Israelis to be quickly defeated, because their defence force had no planes, no heavy artillery, and had to rely on armoured vehicles which they had stolen from the British or built themselves. However, the result was surprising. The Israelis not only defeated the Arab forces, but they won more territory than had been allocated to them by the UN. The Arab countries failed to win because they had soldiers who were often untrained, had little or no combat experience, and had no united command.

The first Arab-Israeli war was really a series of disorganised clashes between small units. There were no conventional front lines and neither side could maintain a long offensive, so most fighting lasted only a few days. The UN was able to set up a truce in June and the UN's mediator, Count Folke Bernadotte, put forward a compromise solution. The Israelis were completely against Bernadotte's plan – the loss of the Negev, Arab rule in Jerusalem, and the return of 300,000 Arab refugees could not be accepted. In September 1948, the Stern Gang assassinated Bernadotte to the horror of the UN and the world. There were many Israelis who felt that the extremists had gone too far and were discrediting the cause of the majority.

▲ Israeli soldiers, armed with a variety of weapons, move up to new positions in July 1948. They are escorted by a home made armoured lorry.

Further fighting broke out in October and the Israelis captured the whole of Galilee. During the following weeks, they pushed the Egyptian forces back into the Sinai desert, leaving the Arabs with a small area of land near Gaza. A new armistice was now agreed through the UN mediator, Ralph Bunche. By the end of the hostilities, more than 700,000 Palestinian Arabs had fled their homeland to live in neighbouring Arab countries.

The Jews had been successful because they were well led. Their soldiers had also had experience of combat in the Second World War, and their guerrilla war against Britain had widened this experience. Above all, the Jews were determined to win – they could not afford to lose. However, after the war, the refugee camps in neighbouring Arab countries became the recruitment grounds for Palestinian freedom fighters. These people would create havoc for the Israelis in the struggle for their own homeland – just as the Israelis had done in their struggle for a homeland against the British.

A stamp issued by the United Arab Republic (Egypt) in 1961 to commemorate Palestine Day. The word on the woman's forehead reads 'Return'.

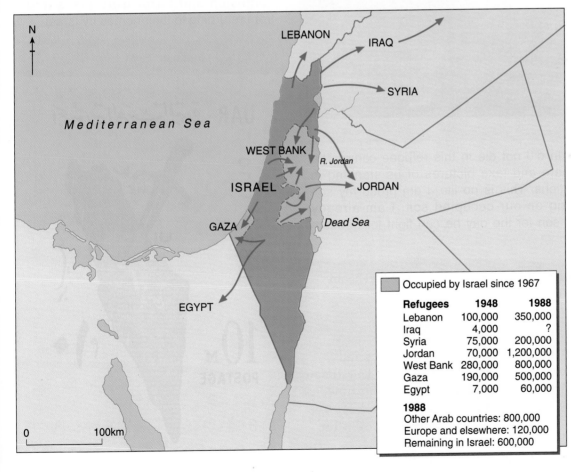

The location and number of Palestinian refugees in 1948 and 1988

Occupied by Israel since 1967		
Refugees	**1948**	**1988**
Lebanon	100,000	350,000
Iraq	4,000	?
Syria	75,000	200,000
Jordan	70,000	1,200,000
West Bank	280,000	800,000
Gaza	190,000	500,000
Egypt	7,000	60,000

1988
Other Arab countries: 800,000
Europe and elsewhere: 120,000
Remaining in Israel: 600,000

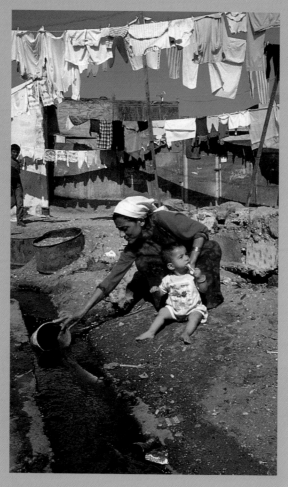

A Palestinian woman and her child collect water from a drainage ditch at a refugee camp on the Gaza Strip in 1993

state. Others believe they decided to leave of their own free will. Investigate the following evidence and make up your own mind.

B

On 9 April 1948 a Zionist force that included elements from Irgun led by Menachem Begin; the Stern Gang led by Yitzhak Shamir; as well as the regular Haganah attacked the peaceful Palestinian Arab village of Deir Yassin near Jerusalem. In cold blood they murdered 154 men, women and children, mutilating many of the bodies. The plan was to frighten the rest of the Palestinian population into leaving to avoid the same happening to them. Thousands of Palestinians who fled during the confusion and terror were prevented from returning to their homes by Israel.

From a PLO pamphlet, 1984.

A

I am proud that my son did not die in this refugee camp. The foreign press come here and take pictures of us standing in queues to get food rations. This is no life. I am proud my son died in action, fighting on our occupied soil. I am already preparing my younger son for the day he can fight for freedom too.

A Palestinian refugee talking about her son just after she had heard about his death in a PLO raid on Israel.

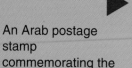
An Arab postage stamp commemorating the Deir Yassin massacre

During 1948 over half of Palestine's Arab population fled their homes and farms. They numbered 726,000 Palestinian Arabs. They and their descendants now live in refugee camps outside Israel.

Controversy surrounds the reasons for these Arabs leaving Palestine. The Palestinians believe that the Jews deliberately terrorised them into leaving in order to seize their land for the new Jewish

C

The affair at Deir Yassin had tremendous effects. The press and radio spread the news everywhere among the Arabs as well as the Jews. In this way a general terror was built up among the Arabs. Driven by fear, the Arabs left their homes to find shelter among their kin. First isolated farms, then villages, and, in the end, whole towns were evacuated.

From the report of the Red Cross official who visited Deir Yassin. He wrote this in 1950.

D

Jewish fighters drive out the inhabitants of the town of Haifa in 1948

E

If the Arabs are so attached to their land, why did they leave it in 1948 during a crisis? The blame must be attributed to Arab leaders who encouraged these Arabs to leave, promising them that after victory in the war they would be able to return to claim the property of the Jews as well. Arab propaganda led them to fear what would happen to them if they stayed, and threatened that they would also be considered traitors to the Arab cause.

From the British-Israeli Public Affairs Committee, which is an official Israeli information service.

F

I next decided to test the charge that the Arab evacuation orders were broadcast by Arab radio. This could be done thoroughly because, in 1948, the BBC monitored all Middle Eastern broadcasts. The records, as well as those done by a US monitoring unit, can be seen at the British Museum.

There was not a single order, or appeal, or suggestion about evacuation from Palestine from any Arab radio station, inside or outside Palestine in 1948.

There is a repeated monitored record of Arab appeals, even flat orders, to the civilians of Palestine to stay put.

From an Irish journalist writing about the Israeli allegations. He wrote this in 1961.

1 Sources B and C suggest some reasons for the Arabs leaving Palestine in 1948. Using only these sources, explain why the Arabs left.
2 Study Sources C and D. In what ways does the evidence of Source C explain the events in the photograph, Source D?
3 Study Sources E and F. In what ways does the evidence of Source F contradict Source E? Refer to the two sources in your answer.
4 How does the author of Source F try to convince you of the reliability of his findings? Does this make the source more useful to a historian?
5 Study Sources B and E. Source B comes from the PLO and Source E is from an Israeli organisation. Does this mean that both these sources are biased? If they are biased, does this make them unreliable as evidence of the events of 1948? Explain your answer.
6 Why did the Palestinian Arabs leave their homes in 1948? Use all of the sources and what you have learned so far from this Chapter to help you answer.

The Suez War, 1956

The Israeli victory and the creation of a Jewish state did not bring an end to the Palestine issue. More than 700,000 Arab refugees were a visible reminder that those who had lost in 1949 were suffering in terrible conditions. The refugee camps became bases for those Palestinian Arabs who wished to fight to expel the Jews from Israel and create their own homeland in Palestine. These Palestinian fighters, called fedayeen, were encouraged by the new President of Egypt, Gamal Abdul Nasser.

War broke out between Egypt and Israel in 1956, but it was a war which had international dimensions. Nasser had developed close links with the USSR, and, in 1955, bought 80 Mig fighters and 45 Ilyushin bombers. Soviet experts were also invited to Egypt to help train Nasser's forces. Relations between Israel and Egypt deteriorated further when the Israeli port of Eilat was blockaded by Egypt at the Gulf of Aqaba. Nasser was surprised that his actions were interpreted by the Americans as allowing the Soviets to move into the Middle East. A promised American loan to build the Aswan Dam was stopped.

The situation then worsened when Nasser nationalized the Suez Canal Company and insisted that he would complete the Aswan Dam using toll revenue from ships using the Canal. The majority shareholders of the Company were Britain and France, and they thought that if Egypt was allowed to control the Canal, then oil supplies could be cut off at will.

What happened after the nationalisation was most surprising. Secret negotiations were held between Britain, France, and Israel and the three countries agreed to create a situation which would allow the combined invasion of Egypt. The invasion would mean that Britain and France could retake the Canal and Israel could destroy the fedayeen bases. The invasion would

also humiliate Nasser and his position as leader of the Arab world would be weakened. However, the scheme did not go according to plan.

The Israeli invasion of Egypt (29 October) was swift and successful, and within days they had captured the Sinai Peninsula, but British and French forces were slow to intervene. Their forces landed on 5 November and were able to seize the Canal with relative ease.

However, world opinion soon turned against Britain and France. The USA opposed their actions because they feared that the Arabs would see the invasion as old style imperialist policy, and, as such, it might mean that the Soviet Union could exploit the situation and increase its own influence in the Middle East. The Soviet Union even threatened military action against Britain, although at the time the Soviets were keen to deflect attention away from their invasion of Hungary. Britain and France were forced to withdraw their forces, to be replaced by UN troops.

Israeli forces advance through the Sinai desert towards the Suez Canal in November 1956

A British tank pauses in a ruined Egyptian street during the Suez invasion

Results of the Suez War

As a result of the Suez War, the Middle East became an area of conflict for the two superpowers and a part of the Cold War. Israel emerged from the war successful once more. The fedayeen bases were destroyed and the border raids stopped. The United Nations sent in an emergency force in the hope that peace could be made long lasting.

For Egypt the results were contradictory. Its armies had been soundly defeated again but, in spite of this, President Nasser emerged a hero with his reputation enhanced. He had shown that he could stand up to Western powers and he could claim that Britain and France had been humiliated because of him.

The Suez War, October-November 1956

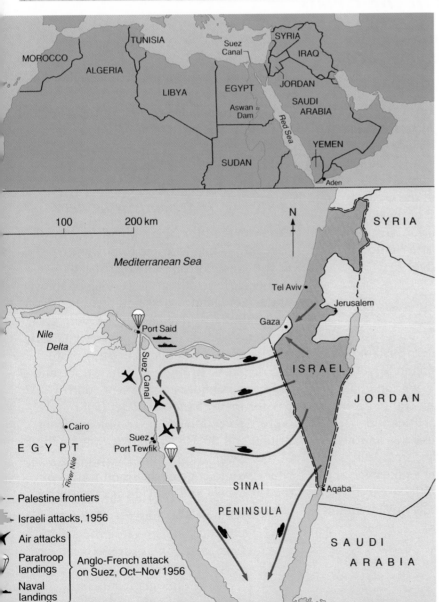

- Palestine frontiers
- Israeli attacks, 1956
- Air attacks
- Paratroop landings
- Naval landings
Anglo-French attack on Suez, Oct–Nov 1956

Suez 1956: Why did it happen then?

Steps towards the crisis

- 1869: Suez Canal opened in Egypt by British and French businessmen.
- 1952: Egyptian revolution. King Farouk abdicated and Egypt became a republic under General Neguib.
- 1954: General Nasser succeeded Neguib as Prime Minister.
- 1955: Nasser agreed to buy weapons from the USSR. This shocked the Western powers.
- 1956: Nasser became President of Egypt.
- July 1956: Britain and the USA refused to lend Egypt any more money.
- July 1956: Nasser took the Suez Canal into Egyptian ownership. He nationalized it.
- 24 October 1956: British, and French Foreign Ministers met secretly in France with the Israeli Prime Minister to decide what to do.
- 29 October 1956: Israeli forces invaded the Sinai peninsula and moved towards Suez.
- 31 October 1956: British and French planes bombed Egyptian airfields.
- 5 November 1956: British and French soldiers landed in Egypt.

Personalities in the Crisis

David Ben-Gurion
Eager to take advantage of the situation?

Ben-Gurion was the Prime Minister of Israel in 1956. (See his biography on page 21). He wanted to teach Egypt and the Arabs a lesson. He wanted to put a stop to the raids on his country from Gaza, stop the Egyptian blockade of the Gulf of Aqaba, and put pressure on Egypt to recognise Israel. Ben-Gurion saw the situation facing Britain and France in 1956 as an opportunity for Israel.

Anthony Eden
Tough on dictators?

Eden was Prime Minister of Britain in 1956. Eden had been Foreign Secretary before the Second World War and had believed in taking a tough stance against the European dictators, Hitler and Mussolini. Eden saw Nasser as another dictator who had to be resisted. When he heard the news of Nasser's take over of the Suez Canal he said, 'I don't care if it's legal or not, he's not going to get away with it.'

In private Eden went further in his opposition to Nasser. He once shouted to an adviser, 'I want him destroyed, don't you understand?'

Eden firmly believed that Britain should not allow Nasser to nationalize the Suez Canal.

President Nasser
A strong, independent leader?

(You can read the biography of Nasser on page 30.) When he came to power in Egypt, Nasser promised great social changes. He set about destroying the power of the large landowners and dividing up the land more fairly. He had to deal with great problems such as disease, poverty and lack of education. His policies became more socialist as he brought industry, trade and newspapers under government control. To pay for these changes, Nasser had to rely on foreign countries. He took loans from Britain and the USA to pay for the building of the Aswan Dam, a massive project which would control the flood waters of the River Nile and provide electricity to a large area of Egypt.

All of this was during the Cold War period. Nasser had refused to join either the US or the Soviet power group. But when Nasser obtained planes and weapons from the USSR this shocked Britain. The British Government stopped its loan of £20 million a year. The USSR then stepped in with money and engineers to help Egypt.

A

I told the French Ambassador that as long as his country supplied Israel with arms, France should supply us as well. Agreement was reached, but France cancelled this two weeks ago. I also asked for arms from the USSR and Czechoslovakia. I told the British and US Ambassadors last June, that if their countries did not supply me with arms I would have to obtain them from the USSR. It was not possible for me to remain silent while Israel imported weapons for her army from several sources and posed a constant threat to us.

From a statement by Nasser on Egypt's arms agreement with Czechoslovakia, September 1955

Nasser was doing what he believed was best for his country, but in doing so he convinced the British that he was placing Egypt against the West and alongside the USSR.

Nasser was confident that he could make Egypt a great Arab country. His fiery speeches calling for Arab unity and the 'liberation' of Palestine were broadcast throughout the Middle East. He was also sure of Egypt's ability to defend itself. He once said, 'Egypt has always been a tomb for invaders.'

B

People of Egypt, we shall maintain our independence and sovereignty. The Suez Canal Company has become our property, and the Egyptian flag flies over it. We shall defend it with our blood and strength, and we shall meet aggression with aggression and evil with evil.
Peace be with you.

From a speech by Nasser justifying the nationalisation of the Suez Canal, July 1956.

Why did it happen then?

Why did the situation in Egypt get to such a point that it became a crisis? Why did that crisis erupt into a war in November 1956?

1   Use the details in this spread and this chapter to analyse the causes of the Suez crisis.
    Make up some cards, about the size of a match box, one for each cause. Don't leave anything out. Now arrange these causes in the following ways:
    a   *Chronological order.* Put out the cards in the order of time in which the events took place. Are there any drawbacks with this method? Are there any overlapping events?
    b   *Long term, short term.* Try to work out which are long term and which are short term causes. Where do you draw the line between long and short term? Do others in the class agree?
    c   *By type.* Place each card under one of the following headings: geographical causes, political causes, economic causes, individuals, chance factors. Which heading has the most cards? Have any cards been left out?
    d   *Order of importance.* Arrange the cards in what you think is their order of importance. Do you agree with others in the class?
2   To help us decide why something happened when it did, it is sometimes useful to remove one factor from a list of causes. What might have happened in November 1956 if the following had not been present?
    a   Nasser
    b   Eden
    c   The Jewish state of Israel
    d   The Cold War between the USA and the USSR

Nasser: Hero or Villain?

Gamal Abdul Nasser

Nasser with Soviet leader Nikita Khrushchev at the opening of the Aswan High Dam

▼ Born 1918
▼ Son of an Alexandria postman
▼ Egyptian army officer
▼ Took part in the revolt against King Farouk in 1952
▼ President of Egypt, 1956-1970
▼ Died 1970

Nasser helped to overthrow King Farouk in 1952; he played a part in negotiating the treaty which led to Britain leaving Egypt after 72 years; and was elected President of Egypt in 1956. Following his decision to nationalize the Suez Canal in 1956, Egypt was invaded by Britain, France, and Israel. Nasser ordered the blocking of the Canal, and, once the invaders were forced to withdraw, Nasser emerged with a greatly enhanced reputation in the Arab world.

In the 1967 War, all of the Sinai Peninsula was occupied by Israel. Nasser accepted responsibility for Egypt's defeat and resigned, but the people took to the streets and demanded his return to government. Nasser died of a heart attack in 1970.

Jubilant Nasser and crowds of Egyptians celebrate following the withdrawal of British soldiers from Egypt

B

Perhaps no other person who figures in the Arab-Israeli conflict has had such different interpretations written about them. Read the following sources and decide for yourself.

A

Nasser was the leading Arab statesman of his age and is remembered for restoring Arab dignity after years of humiliation by the West.

From an American reference book, 1995.

Grabber Nasser.
Nasser is the Boss leader of Egypt. But he has chosen a crude and dangerous method to show that he is a Big Shot. Remember Adolf Hitler? He ended by burning in a petrol-soaked blanket outside his bunker in the heart of devastated Berlin.

From a British newsapaper, *The Daily Mirror*, printed in July 1956.

'I have never thought of Nasser as a Hitler, but the similarity to Mussolini is close.'

'Our quarrel is not with Egypt, it is with Nasser. Instead of meeting us with friendship, Nasser conducted a vicious propaganda campaign against us. He has shown that he is not a man who can be trusted. We all know how dictatorships behave, and we all remember what the cost was of giving in to Hitler.'

Two quotes from British Prime Minister Anthony Eden, speaking about Nasser in 1956.

A British cartoonist shows Nasser in 1956 looking remarkably like Hitler

Study Sources A and B.
1   What interpretation of Nasser is given in Source A?
2   In what ways does Source B support Source A? Explain your answer.
3   Study Sources C and D.
    Compare the value of these two sources as evidence of British public opinion of Nasser at the time of the Suez crisis.
4   What interpretation of Nasser is given by Sources C, D, and E?
5   The sources in this feature give very different interpretations of President Nasser. Was Nasser a hero or was he a villain? Or is there a third, more balanced, interpretation of the Egyptian leader? Use the evidence in this spread, together with what you have learned from the rest of this chapter, to explain your thoughts about Nasser up to the Suez War.

The Six Day War, 1967

The United Nations were unable to keep the peace for long. Eleven years after the Suez War another war erupted. Israel had continued to build up its armed forces by purchasing supplies from Britain, France, the USA, and West Germany; the Arab states were supplied by the USSR.

Despite the presence of the United Nations, border skirmishes continued between the Israelis and the Palestinian guerrilla groups. Groups such as Fatah and the Palestine Liberation Organisation were a constant problem for the Israeli security forces and those who lived in settlements near the borders.

By 1967, Nasser felt that the Arab forces were strong enough to defeat Israel. In May, Nasser ordered the UN forces out of Egypt and he then closed the Gulf of Aqaba to Israel, blockading the port of Eilat. There were also troop movements near Israel's borders with Lebanon, Syria, and Jordan (whose forces were supplemented by Iraqi, Saudi Arabian and Algerian troops).

▲ This Lebanese cartoon from May 1967 shows Israel squeezed between the military forces of her Arab neighbours

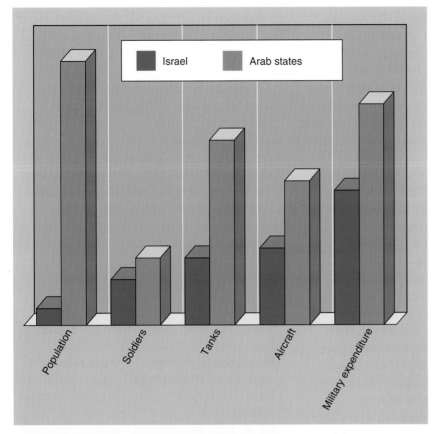

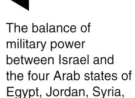

The balance of military power between Israel and the four Arab states of Egypt, Jordan, Syria, and Iraq in 1967

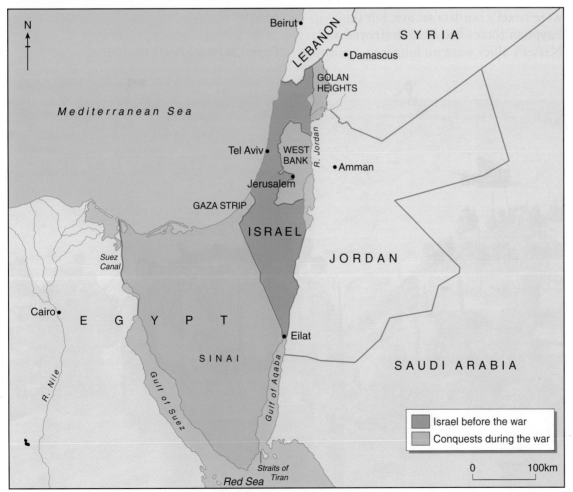

Territory gained by Israel during the Six Day War, 1967

However, without waiting to be attacked, the Israelis launched an attack against their enemies on 5 June. The fighting was over in six days, after which Israel had maintained and expanded its borders, and had greater security than ever before. Using surprise shock tactics, the Israelis were able to destroy their enemies' air forces on the ground – they lost only 26 aircraft compared with 400 by the Arab countries. The Egyptians were pushed back through the Sinai desert and huge numbers of tanks were destroyed at the Mitla pass. The Israelis then secured their border by occupying the Gaza Strip.

In the north, the Syrians were also defeated and the Israelis captured the Golan Heights. It was just the same in the fighting against Jordan, where the West Bank of the River Jordan was captured. But most important of all for the Israelis, the eastern part of Jerusalem was at last captured. Their holy city was now completely under their control. The victory was stunning and comprehensive. Not only were Israel's borders secure, but the Egyptian forces had been destroyed and Nasser's allies were no longer in a position to threaten Israel. The victory was so swift that there had been little chance for world opinion to influence the outcome of the war.

Once again, victory did not mean the end of the conflict. There was a further surge of refugees into the camps, swelling numbers to about 1.5 million. The Israelis were at the height of their success, but the Palestinian Arabs refused to accept defeat.

In November 1967, the United Nations passed Resolution 242 which was to become the basis of Palestinian demands in the future.

i Withdrawal of Israel from the occupied territories
ii Acknowledgement of the sovereignty and territorial integrity and political independence of every state in the Middle East
iii A just settlement to the refugee problem

From UN Resolution 242, 1967.

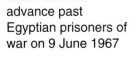

Israeli soldiers advance past Egyptian prisoners of war on 9 June 1967

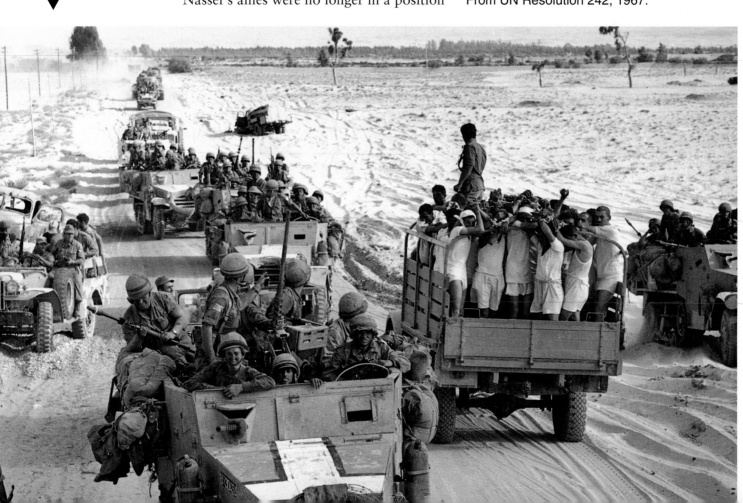

Moshe Dayan

Moshe Dayan enters East Jerusalem in 1967. He said 'We have unified Jerusalem, the divided capital of Israel. We have returned to the Holiest of our Holy places, never to part from it again.'

▼ Born 1915
▼ Arrested by the British in 1939
▼ Military career in the British and Israeli armies until 1958
▼ Israeli Defence Minister 1966-1974
▼ Died 1981

Dayan was born on a Kibbutz in Israel and, at the age of 14, he began his military career when he joined the Haganah to defend Jewish settlements from Arab attacks. Later he was given special guerrilla training by the British, but, when the Haganah was outlawed, Dayan was arrested by the British. He was released in 1941 and fought with the British army in the Second World War. Dayan was commander of the Israeli forces on the Jerusalem front in 1948-9 and became Chief of the General Staff in 1953. He left the army in 1958 and was elected to the Knesset (Israeli Parliament) a year later. In 1966 Dayan became Israeli Defence Minister and took the credit for successes in the Six Day War of 1967.

But six years later, Dayan was criticised for Israel's unpreparedness in the Yom Kippur War of 1973 and he resigned in 1974. Later, as Foreign Minister in Menachem Begin's government, Dayan played a part in negotiating the peace treaty with Egypt in 1979. He resigned from politics in 1979 and died two years later.

For 25 years Moshe Dayan, the soldier with the famous eye patch, was a symbol of Israel's determination and will to survive.

The 1967 War: Why did it happen then?

After the Suez War of 1956, Arab nationalism grew dramatically. So did the demands for revenge led by Egypt's President Nasser. The formation of a united Arab military command that massed soldiers and tanks along the borders with Israel, and the closing of the Gulf of Aqaba, worried Israel. Then, in May 1967, Nasser insisted that the United Nations removed its forces from Egypt. This was followed by speeches in which Nasser gave away his intention to take control of the Gulf of Aqaba and support the Palestinians.

'Under no circumstances will we allow the Israeli flag to pass through the Gulf of Aqaba.'

'The issue now at hand is not the Gulf of Aqaba, the Straits of Tiran, or the withdrawal of the United Nations forces, but the rights of the Palestinian people. It is the aggression which took place in Palestine in 1948 with the collaboration of Britain and the United States of America.'

From speeches given by President Nasser in May 1967.

On 5 June Israeli forces attacked Egypt, Jordan, and Syria, taking them almost completely by surprise. Six days later Israel had won an almost complete victory.

Make sure that you have read through the part of this chapter on the causes of the Six Day War before you attempt these questions. Now read the following list of causes of the Six Day War.

- Egypt's blockade of the Gulf of Aqaba
- Fatah and PLO raids on Israel
- The creation of an independent, Jewish Israel.
- Israel's decision to strike first in June 1967
- Expulsion of UN forces from Egypt

1. Add at least one more cause to the list.
2. Sort the causes in the list into chronological order, add in dates where you can.
3. Arrange the causes into two lists, showing the long term and short term causes of the Six Day War.
4. Choose any two of the causes and explain in detail how they link together.
5. Which do you think was the most important cause of the Six Day War? Explain your answer referring to the evidence.
6. 'Israel and Egypt are equally to blame for the outbreak of war in June 1967.' Use the evidence from this chapter and this page to explain whether you agree or disagree with this statement.

The Yom Kippur War, 1973

There was an uneasy peace in the years after 1967. The Israelis built Jewish settlements on the West Bank and in Sinai. Such action inflamed the situation. It was a time when the Palestine Liberation Organisation (see page 44) emerged and attracted the attention of the world by activities such as hijacking aeroplanes and kidnapping high ranking officials. The Egyptians and Syrians were determined to avenge the defeats of the three previous wars and made secret preparations to attack Israel. The new Egyptian President, Anwar Sadat, had received extensive military aid from the USSR and the Egyptian troops were better trained than in the previous wars.

On 6 October 1973, Egyptian forces crossed the Suez Canal and captured territory in the Sinai desert. At the same time, the Syrians attacked Israel at the Golan Heights. The two countries had made a secret plan to invade and had attacked on one of Israel's most sacred days – the religious festival of Yom Kippur. This was a national holiday for Israel and its armed forces were taken completely by surprise. The startled Israelis were unable to gain air superiority, as they had in 1967, because the Egyptians were able to use the advanced technology of the USSR with surface to air missiles (SAMs). The SAMs were based on the west side of the Suez Canal and they acted as a shield for the Egyptian land forces. There were even portable SAMs which increased the power and confidence of the Egyptians.

Portable Egyptian SAM missiles in the Sinai Desert, 1973

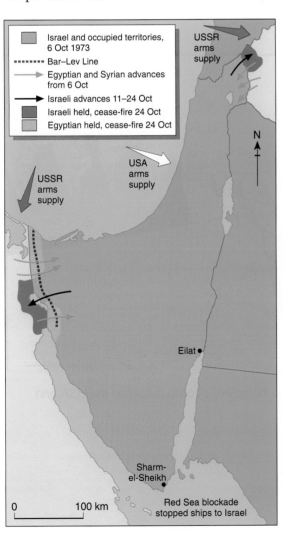

The Yom Kippur War, 1973

The Israelis decided to concentrate on pushing the Syrians back and tried to prevent the Egyptians from advancing further into the Sinai. By 12 October, the Golan Heights had been recaptured and the Israelis were able to move troops from the north to the Sinai front. Perhaps the biggest mistake of the war was the movement of Egyptian forces beyond the cover of the SAMs – as soon as this happened the Israeli forces crushed the Egyptians at the Mitla Pass and began to push them back to the Canal.

The Israelis then made a daring counter-attack. They crossed the Suez Canal, captured some of the SAM bases and began to move on Cairo, the Egyptian capital. The Egyptian forces found themselves stranded on the Sinai side of the Canal.

It was at this stage that the war took on some different features from the earlier wars. In this war the Arab states used oil as a weapon. The oil producing countries of the Arab Gulf were members of the Organisation of Petroleum Exporting Countries (OPEC) and they now decided to use oil as an economic weapon against Israel and its Western allies. The price of oil was raised by 70% and Saudi Arabia cut its production by 10%. No oil was to be exported to the USA. The threat to the oil supplies of the West made the Western politicians realise the enormity of the situation. The economies of Western Europe and the USA would be severely disrupted if the war was to last for a long time. Intense diplomacy therefore began at the height of the conflict.

Yet again the conflict between the Arabs and the Israelis had taken on international

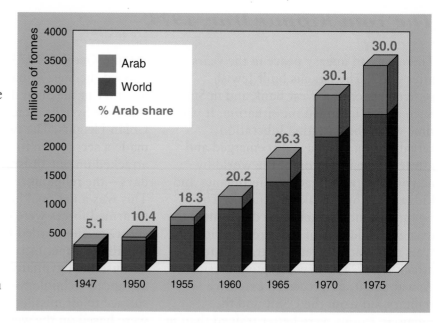

▲ World oil production figures, showing the growing influence of the Middle East

▲ The Arab states use the power of oil to influence the USA and Western Europe

dimensions. The USA, the USSR, and the UN each put pressure on the combatants and a ceasefire was reached on 24 October. It was difficult to see who had won. The war had shown that the Israelis were not unbeatable and the Arab armies had been able to regain some of their lost pride. The Israelis could point to some successes because they had pushed both the Egyptians and Syrians back after their initial advances. Both Israel and Egypt now seemed to realise that there could never be a lasting peace unless each was prepared to make concessions.

Losses in the Yom Kippur War

	Killed	Tanks destroyed
Israel	2,800	250
Egypt	11,000	700
Syria	c5,000	1,150

 B

> i All parties concerned are to start the implementation of Security Council Resolution 242 in all of its parts [see page 34]
> ii All parties concerned should start negotiations aimed at establishing a just and lasting peace in the Middle East.

From UN Resolution 338 passed on 22 October 1973.

1 Describe:
  a the differences, and
  b the similarities between the Yom Kippur War and the three previous Arab-Israeli wars.
2 It is difficult to see who won the war of Yom Kippur. Write a newspaper report from either an Arab or an Israeli point of view, showing how your side had done well in the war.

▲ Golda Meir with her Defence Minister, Moshe Dayan

Golda Meir

▼ Born 1898 in the Ukraine
▼ Emigrated to the USA in 1906, then to Palestine in 1921
▼ Elected to Israel's first Knesset, where she served until 1974
▼ Prime Minister 1969-1974
▼ Died 1978

Meir became a Zionist when she was in her teens, and became dedicated to building a home for the Jews. In 1921 she and her husband emigrated to Palestine. Golda Meir was active in Jewish politics during the 1920s and 1930s and she became Labour Minister in the first Israeli government. Meir was Prime Minister from 1969 to 1974, when she resigned because of the controversy which followed Israel's lack of readiness in the 1973 Yom Kippur War.

Why was the Israeli army so successful?

In the wars of 1948, 1956, and 1967 the Israeli armed forces were stunningly successful. Against the numerically superior forces of Egypt, Jordan, and Syria the Israeli army and air force gained success after success.

Why was this so?

Though they seemed low on numbers in 1948, the Israeli defence forces were in fact very well prepared for war. David Ben-Gurion (see page 21) was one of those who had welded together various groups into the Israeli army. The Haganah was the official Jewish militia, formed with British help to enable the Jews in Palestine to defend themselves against attacks from Arabs. These fighters were given special anti-guerrilla training by British experts such as Orde Wingate. Moshe Dayan, who was to become a top Israeli General and later the Defence Minister, was trained by the British when he was in the Haganah.

During the Second World War, thousands of Jews were trained, equipped and fought with the British army in Jewish Brigades. Then there was the Palmach, a group of Jewish fighters who fought against the British until 1947. Yitzhak Rabin (see page 72) was a member of Palmach.

After the Second World War a number of Jews who had fought against the German army in Eastern Europe or in the resistance armies in France and Italy made their way to Palestine. These were experienced and sometimes ruthless fighters, men and women who had seen the worst of Nazi brutality at first hand and who were now determined to fight for a Jewish homeland. They included many of those who later led Israel, such as Menachem Begin (see page 57) and Yitzhak Shamir. They formed groups such as Irgun and the Stern Gang, which fought against the British, attacked the Arab settlement at Deir Yassin, and then fought against the Arab armies which attacked Israel in 1948.

Their determination to build the Jewish state, and to make certain of its survival, was a factor in the continued strength of the Israeli armed forces. They began with an assortment of weapons stolen from the British or bought cheaply after the Second World War. Israel also introduced compulsory military service for its young men and women to ensure that the army always had a good supply of trained soldiers.

▲ Men of the Jewish militia, Haganah, specially trained by Orde Wingate, a British expert in guerrilla warfare, at their base in Palestine, 1939

Israeli soldiers from border settlements march past during a big military parade in Jerusalem marking Israel's 17th Independence Day

Meanwhile, Israeli politicians worked hard to gain the recognition of other countries and to buy weapons from them. This policy resulted in arms deals with France and later the USA. By 1967 Israel was better armed than its Arab neighbours.

Israel has also always had excellent military leaders. The best known of these was Moshe Dayan, who was Chief of Staff of his country's army in the war of 1956, and Defence Minister during the Six Day War of 1967 (see page 35).

1 List the reasons for the success of the Israeli army given in this section.
2 Which of these reasons do you think is the most important? Explain your choice.
3 Show how the reason you have selected helps to explain the success of the Israeli army in the war of 1948, 1956, or 1967.

4 Continuing the struggle: the Palestinians from diaspora to the Intifada

An Arab refugee camp near the Dead Sea in 1949

There was no such thing as Palestinians. It is not as though there was a Palestinian people and we came and threw them out and took their country from them. They did not exist.

Golda Meir, Prime Minister of Israel, 1969.

The Zionists consider the Arabs who live in the occupied territories to be a backward people unworthy of equality of rights or of treatment and undeserving of justice. It is now the Israelis who lay down the study courses for Arab schools.

The learning of Hebrew is compulsory for all Arab pupils. The number of teachers in Arab schools is very few and the school equipment is deplorable. The Arabs are prevented from forming political parties.

An extract from *Zionism – a racist expansionist movement*, published by the Arab League in 1969.

Sources A and B indicate that the Palestinian Arabs have suffered greatly in the conflict with Israel. The creation of a Jewish state in 1948, as you have already seen in Chapter 2, led to over 700,000 Palestinian Arabs fleeing what they considered to be their homeland. In the first conflict of 1948-49, the bulk of the refugees went to the Gaza Strip and the West Bank, though many also went to neighbouring states (see page 23).

The United Nations issued a Resolution which said that the Palestinian refugees should be allowed to return at the earliest possible date or be given compensation if they chose not to return. Israel ignored the Resolution.

There were distinct problems for those countries to which the Palestinians fled. Should the Palestinians be provided with decent housing, education, health facilities etc? Most countries were unable to afford to do so. Also if the refugees were absorbed into the host nation, and stopped being 'Palestinians', then the Israelis had 'won'. Therefore, the camps became permanent and the vast majority of refugees remained in them.

The United Nations did step in to provide food and some welfare services but, apart from this humanitarian assistance, the UN has been unable to find a solution to the refugee problem. There were many in the refugee camps who came to believe that the only way to regain Palestine was by force. In the 1950s, groups of activists, calling themselves 'fedayeen' (self-sacrificers), began to attack Israeli settlements (see page 26). By early 1964, the Palestinians had become well organised and drew up their National Covenant.

Article One:
   Palestine is an Arab homeland bound by strong Arab National ties to the rest of the Arab countries and which together form the large Arab homeland.
Article Three:
   The Palestinian people have a legitimate right to their homeland.
Article Six:
   The Palestinians are those Arab citizens who were living in Palestine up to 1947, whether they remained or were expelled. Every child who was born to a Palestinian parent after this date whether in Palestine or outside is a Palestinian.
Article Seven:
   Jews of Palestinian origin are considered Palestinians if they are willing to live peacefully and loyally in Palestine.

From the Palestinian National Covenant, May 1964.

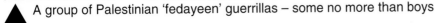 A group of Palestinian 'fedayeen' guerrillas – some no more than boys

One of the first Palestinian groups to employ guerrilla tactics against Israel was the Palestine National Liberation Movement, also known as Fatah. This organisation was founded by Yasser Arafat in 1958 and it grew in importance during the next ten years. The Palestine Liberation Organisation was formed in 1964 and it claimed that the creation of Israel had been an injustice and that the land rightly belonged to the Arabs. The PLO aimed to unite the Palestinian refugees and regain the land that had been lost to the Israelis. When Israel defeated the Arab countries in the Six Day War, the activities of the PLO and other groups increased.

A turning point for the PLO came in 1968 when its forces were able to resist Israeli troops at Karameh. Here, the Israelis lost many tanks and aeroplanes. The success of the PLO encouraged many thousands of Palestinians to join the various armed groups at a time when hopes were faint following the Israeli victory in the 1967 war. The other key event for the PLO was the appointment of Yasser Arafat as its Chairman.

Abu Jihad (Khalil Alwazir).
A leading Palestinian nationalist. In 1958 Jihad and Yasser Arafat formed the Palestine National Liberation Movement. Because it was a crime to assert their Palestinian identity openly, they decided to work in secret to organise into a resistance movement. He is pictured here in 1978.

Camouflaged Palestinian snipers pictured before going into action in Israel

The PLO adopted methods which it thought would terrorize Israel into giving up the conquered lands. There were hijackings of aeroplanes, kidnappings and bombings, together with raids on Israeli settlements. These actions did not persuade Israel to go to the negotiating table. Rather it simply spurred them to acts of retaliation – they too bombed enemy bases, and, because these bases were in or near refugee camps, there were often many civilian casualties.

The activities of the PLO continued and reached a climax in September 1970. Five aircraft were hijacked and three of the planes were taken to an old RAF airstrip at Dawson's Field in Jordan. The PLO demanded the release of certain prisoners and Britain, West Germany, and Switzerland agreed to the demands. However, the PLO then blew up the three aeroplanes, an act which shocked the world. The actions of the PLO had also concerned King Hussein of Jordan because he feared foreign intervention after these hijackings. He decided that the time had come to rid Jordan of the PLO. A fierce conflict broke out and, after several days fighting, Arafat and the PLO were pushed out of Jordan and set up new headquarters in Lebanon (see page 61). More than 10,000 PLO supporters were killed in the fighting.

King Hussein makes a tour of the front line areas in Jordan in 1969

King Hussein of Jordan

▼ Born 1935
▼ Educated in Jordan, Egypt, and Britain
▼ Gave up his country's claim to the West Bank in 1988
▼ Signed a peace accord with Israel in 1994

Hussein became King of Jordan in 1952. Many Palestinian refugees had settled in his country in 1948, and more arrived there after the 1967 Six Day War. The PLO had a great deal of power in Jordan, and in 1970 Hussein's soldiers were successful in forcing out the Palestinian guerrillas.

In 1988, following months of demonstrations by Palestinians in the West Bank, King Hussein gave up all Jordanian claims to the West Bank.

Following the signing of a peace accord between Israel and the PLO in 1993, Hussein, as head of the Arab nation with the highest concentration of Palestinian refugees, stated Jordan's right to play a part in the peace process, and in 1994 a peace accord was signed between Israel and Jordan.

Hussein accompanied Yasser Arafat to the USA for peace talks and, in 1997, visited Israel to console the families of Israeli children killed by a Jordanian soldier (see pages 4 and 75).

The roots of the Palestine question do not stem from any conflict between two religions or two nationalisms. Neither is it a border conflict between two neighbouring states. It is the cause of a people deprived of its homeland, dispersed and uprooted, living mostly in exile and in refugee camps... Today I have come bearing an olive branch and a freedom fighter's gun. Do not let the olive branch fall from my hand.

An extract from Yasser Arafat's speech to the United Nations, 1974.

The diplomacy of Henry Kissinger of the USA (see page 54) after the Yom Kippur War (1973) did re-establish some hope for the future. The PLO seemed to become more moderate after this war, and, in November 1974, Yasser Arafat was invited to speak at the United Nations (see Source D and the photograph on page 48).

Many countries were beginning to sympathize with Arafat and the Palestinians, but there were some who agreed with Israel that negotiations could not begin until the PLO renounced violence. When the Camp David Accord was signed (see page 55), it seemed as if the Palestinians were being left behind as Egypt made its own peace settlement. When the Israelis invaded Lebanon in 1982 and expelled the PLO (see pages 59–60), Arafat and his supporters had to regroup once more.

Events in Lebanon seemed to show that the Palestinians were making no progress in their quest for a homeland. The expulsion of the PLO from Lebanon caused a split in the leadership and some leaders were now prepared to accept a smaller Palestinian state. Those who disagreed wished to continue the armed struggle against Israel, and the extremists carried out many attacks which did raise the profile of the Palestinian problem but did little to bring a solution.

Guerrilla activities against Israel continued, and, in 1987, the Palestinians began the Intifada in the occupied territories. The Intifada (uprising) saw civil disobedience grow in Gaza and the West Bank. There were riots and protests and schools were closed. The Israeli Defence Minister announced a policy of 'force, might and beatings' against Palestinians who joined the uprising. Eventually the Israelis discovered that the way to minimize trouble was to use undercover units to target specific individuals. The severe Israeli reaction was caught on the world's television and cost Israel a lot of international support.

Two forms of Palestinian protest. Palestinians in the occupied territories throw stones at Israeli soldiers during the Intifada in 1990. Below, Palestinians who still live in Israel demonstrate peacefully in 1988.

The Intifada continued into the 1990s, but it was at this time that one major event changed the situation in the Middle East. In August 1990, Saddam Hussein invaded Kuwait and the Gulf War began. Yasser Arafat supported Saddam Hussein. This decision proved crucial, because those Arab countries which had previously supported the PLO and given it shelter and money, opposed Saddam and now cut off support for the PLO.

The financial losses of the PLO were huge. The loss of annual donations from Saudi Arabia and Kuwait cost it $120 million, and confiscations of Palestinian deposits in Kuwaiti banks, plus the loss of other revenues, brought PLO losses from the Gulf states to about $10 billion in the years 1991-93. This reduction in funding meant that the PLO had to close missions abroad and suspend educational, welfare, and social services for Palestinian refugees. The Gulf states added to the refugee problem by expelling 400,000 Palestinians who worked there. The PLO's future looked bleak.

Yasser Arafat

▲

Yasser Arafat gives a speech to the UN General Assembly in 1974. The empty seats in the front row belong to the Israeli delegation.

▼ Born 1929, Jerusalem
▼ Left Jerusalem soon after the creation of the Israeli state
▼ Leader of the PLO since 1968
▼ Signed peace accords with Israeli leaders in the mid 1990s
▼ Won Nobel Peace Prize, 1994

Arafat left Palestine to study engineering in Egypt, but at the same time was training as a fedayeen commando. In 1958 he set up Fatah and led fedayeen raids into Israel. Arafat linked Fatah with similar groups in the PLO and became leader of the PLO in 1968. He has worked to gain international recognition for the PLO.

Since the 1980s, Arafat has tried hard to change his image from that of freedom fighter to moderate statesman. In 1988 he recognised the right of Israel to exist, which led to talks with the Israeli leaders. In 1993, following secret negotiations in Norway, Arafat signed a Peace Accord with Yitzhak Rabin, the leader of Israel. This was followed in 1997 by an Accord signed with Benjamin Netanyahu.

Arafat's approach has gained home rule for Palestinian Arabs in Gaza and Jericho, but he has had to face extreme criticism from groups such as Hamas and Hezbollah, for betraying Palestinian claims to full independence.

As the Intifada lost some of its impetus, a new faction appeared – the Islamic Resistance Movement or Hamas. Hamas was independent of the PLO and soon became a powerful force in the occupied territories. It rejected the Madrid talks (see page 63), and claimed that the PLO did not represent all the Palestinians. Hamas and the PLO openly opposed each other, and, in July 1992, street battles between their supporters in Gaza left 3 dead and 100 injured. When Hamas killed 6 Israeli soldiers in December 1992, the Israeli government reacted by expelling more than 400 suspected Hamas supporters and abandoned them in southern Lebanon. There then began the worst period of violence since the start of the Intifada. The occupied territories were closed off and 189,000 Palestinians were prevented from working. Between February and May 1993, Israeli defence forces killed 67 Palestinians in the Gaza Strip and wounded 1,552. Property damage amounted to $50 million. By the time of the secret Oslo peace talks (see page 63), there were 17,000 Palestinians in Israeli prisons, and most of them had been imprisoned during the previous nine months.

Almost six years after the Intifada began, it seemed as if there was some clear progress, but, yet again, the situation had changed. The PLO was not as strong as it had been, and the emergence of Hamas meant that there would be a large number of Palestinians who would not accept a compromise solution with Israel.

1 Describe the problems the Palestinian refugees caused in the countries to which they fled.
2 Why did King Hussein expel the PLO from Jordan?
3 Read Sources A and C. In what ways do these sources give you different interpretations about the Palestinian people?
4 Read Source D. What does Arafat mean when he says "I have come bearing an olive branch and a freedom fighter's gun"?
5 In what ways have the Palestinians attempted to win back their homeland in the years between 1949 and 1991?
6 Use all the sources and the information in this chapter to explain why the Palestinians might want to go to the "negotiating table" referred to in Source E.

You [the Palestinian delegation] want to solve the problem? The place to do that is around the negotiating table. So it is permissible to keep the [occupied] territories closed as long as possible.

Yitzhak Rabin, Prime Minister of Israel, April 1993.

The Palestine Liberation Organisation was set up in 1964. Its guerrilla army is called Fatah. Fighters of Fatah and the PLO have been described as:

- ◆ Freedom fighters
- ◆ Guerrillas
- ◆ Terrorists
- ◆ Murderers

As well as being descriptive, each of these terms has a definite meaning and makes a judgement. Which words we choose to describe Fatah and the PLO depends very much on how we see them and the judgements we make of them. In other words, we are forced to make our interpretation of them.

Study the sources in this feature and then answer the questions which follow.

A

C Palestinian guerrillas learn how to lay mines

D

For twenty years our people have been waiting for a just solution to the Palestinian problem. All that we got was charity and humiliation while others continue to live in our homes. I refuse to remain a refugee. I have decided to join the freedom fighters and I ask for your blessing.

From a letter by a Palestinian student in Beirut, Lebanon, to his parents, 1968.

B

Yasser Arafat, the leader of the PLO, receiving the Nobel Peace Prize along with Shimon Peres and Yitzhak Rabin of Israel in December 1994.

At no time did the Palestinians develop a nationality of their own or try to achieve independence. Champions of the Arabs claim that the Jews took "their country" away from them. In reality no such country existed.

Terence Prittie, a British writer.

E

Arafat and most of the leaders of the PLO wanted to limit raids and bombings to Israeli territory because their military aim was strictly war on Israel. However, some extremist Palestinian groups caused a division inside the PLO by making attacks in other parts of the world. They were impatient and were not prepared to wait ten or twenty years. These Palestinians realised that raids into Israel achieved little.

From a British history book written in 1984.

F

Palestine is our country
  Our aim is to return

Death does not frighten us
  Palestine is ours

We shall never forget her
  *Another homeland we shall
  never accept!*

Our Palestine, witness,
  O God and history
  *We promise to shed
  our blood for you!*

A Palestinian poem.

G

'When we hijack a plane it has more effect than if we killed a hundred Israelis in battle. For decades world public opinion has been neither for nor against the Palestinians. It simply ignored us. At least the world is talking about us now.'

'The non-violent methods are very beautiful and very easy, and we wish we could win with these methods. Our people do not carry machine-guns and bombs because they enjoy killing. It is a last resort. For twenty-two years we waited for the United Nations and the United States, for liberty, for freedom and democracy. There was no result. So this is our last resort.'

Two quotes from interviews with PLO members in the early 1970s.

1 In Source A the student calls himself a freedom fighter. How might the author of Source B describe him?

2 In what ways do the evidence of Sources B and F disagree?

3 Look at Sources D and E. What impression do these two sources give of Yasser Arafat?

4 According to the authors of Sources A and G, why have the Palestinians used violent methods?

5 Do Sources E and G support the evidence of Source D? Explain your answer with reference to the sources.

6 What doubts might a historian of the Arab-Israeli conflict have about using the following sources as evidence:
   a the views of PLO members, such as those in Sources A and G?

   b the statements of writers such as the authors of Sources B and E?
   Explain the reasons for any doubts you think of.

7 Does your answer to question 6 mean that Sources A, B, E, and G are of little or no use to an historian of the conflict? Explain your answer fully.

Research and extended writing task.

Write a balanced account of the development of the PLO up to 1994. Use this book, together with any other information you can find. You should be aware that everything you read about the PLO is an interpretation and may be biased. Try to be as unbiased as possible in your own writing, taking care over the words you select to describe the PLO.

The use of violence.

Three aircraft hijacked by the PLO are blown up at Dawson's Field, 1970

A
Arab aircraft destroyed in an Israeli raid, Beirut Airport, 1968

Massacre 1948

At 5 am on 10 April 1948, the Arab village of Deir Yassin, outside Jerusalem, was the target of a Jewish attack. Irgun fighters, led by Menachem Begin, advanced on the waking villagers. By noon they had killed all of the 254 inhabitants – men, women and children. This act spread panic amongst the Arabs. Sami Hadawi, a Jewish soldier in 1948, wrote:

'Most of the men had left the village. The irregular Jewish troops shot every one they saw in the houses, including women and children. Twenty five men had been brought out of the houses. They were taken to a stone quarry and shot in cold blood.'

Massacre 1972

On 5 September 1972, Palestinian guerrillas attacked the Israeli athletes who were competing at the Olympic Games in Munich, Germany. They killed two athletes on the spot and held others hostage. They then demanded that 200 Palestinians in Israeli prisons be released. The German police decided to attempt a rescue. Nine more athletes were killed by the PLO. The headline in *The London Evening Standard* read:

'Murder at the Olympics.
Arab terrorists gun down Israelis in Munich village – 13 held as hostages.'

A few days later the Israelis took revenge by killing over 200 Palestinian refugees in Syria and Lebanon.

Massacre 1982

1000 refugees in the Palestinian refugee camps in Sabra and Chatila in Lebanon were killed by members of the Lebanese Christian militia, the allies of Israel. A western journalist in Lebanon wrote:

'The victims were men, women and children of all ages, from the very old to the very young, even babies in arms. They were killed in every possible way. The lucky ones were shot, singly or in groups. Others were strangled or had their throats slit. They were mutilated, before or after death; genitals and breasts were sliced off'

1 What are the similarities between Sources A and B, and between Sources C, D, and E?
2 Can you point out any differences between these sources?

When we look at the Arab-Israeli conflict over a period of time, we can see a large number of similarities in the way violence has been used by each side. For example, each side has its own army or fighters, and each side has been prepared to be utterly ruthless in the use of violence.

As well as the kind of violence illustrated in Sources A-E, which has been used by Israel and the PLO, there have also been a number of wars between Israel and its Arab neighbours.

Wars between Israel and its Arab Neighbours.

1948 *War*
   1956 *Suez War*
      1967 *Six Day War*
         1973 *War of Yom Kippur*

3 Why has there been so much violence in the Arab-Israeli conflict?

5 *A*n uneasy peace, 1973–1993

Israel soon realised that the position of the USA changed after the Yom Kippur War. The oil weapon proved to be the Arabs' greatest ally, for the West depended on oil and the price rises of 1973 had caused economic recession very quickly. The USA still wished to support Israel but could not afford to offend the Arab countries. There were several million Jews in the USA and many sent money to support Israel. They were a powerful pressure group and could not be ignored by the President, therefore, peace in the Middle East soon became the goal of successive American Presidents.

Henry Kissinger, the National Security Adviser of President Nixon, attempted to bring some peace and stability to the Middle East. Kissinger travelled tirelessly between Cairo, Tel Aviv, and Damascus in the cause of peace. This was called shuttle diplomacy. Kissinger arranged ceasefire agreements between the warring countries and helped to set up Middle East peace talks at Geneva. The peace talks at Geneva opened in December 1973, and this was the first time that Arabs and Israelis had sat together at a peace conference. In January 1974, Egypt and Israel agreed to withdraw their forces on the Suez Canal, and, in May, Syria and Israel agreed to separate their forces on the Golan Heights. UN troops were brought in to keep Egypt and Israel apart. President Nixon visited the Middle East, and this seemed to symbolize changes in US policy indicating a desire for better relations with Arab countries.

▲

This cartoon, published by the *Daily Mail* in October 1973, shows Henry Kissinger and President Nixon of the USA negotiating with Egypt

Henry Kissinger

▼ Born 1923
▼ American scholar, statesman, and Secretary of State to two Presidents
▼ Nobel Peace Prize winner in 1973
▼ Negotiated an agreement between Egypt and Israel in 1974

Kissinger was born in Germany, but was taken to the USA by his parents in 1938 and fought in the US army, as an ordinary soldier, during the Second World War. In 1973 Kissinger managed to negotiate a cease-fire in Vietnam, which earned him a Nobel Peace Prize. He became Secretary of State in 1973 and negotiated an agreement between Egypt and Israel in 1974, a forerunner of the Camp David Agreement. Kissinger tried, but was unsuccessful, in finding a solution to the problems facing South Africa.

◀

Henry Kissinger and Anwar Sadat of Egypt in 1975

Peace talks began between the two countries in 1978 and, when they ran into difficulties, President Carter offered to act as mediator and invited Sadat and Begin to his holiday home at Camp David. Talks at Camp David lasted for thirteen days and agreement was eventually reached and signed at the White House. In the Camp David Accords, Sadat and Begin agreed to negotiate a peace treaty and establish diplomatic relations. Egypt would recognise Israel's right to exist. In return Israel would gradually withdraw from the Sinai Peninsula and return it to Egypt. Begin and Sadat also pledged to start talks on Palestinian self-rule. After a difficult round of negotiations, both nations signed a peace treaty in Washington DC on 26 March 1979. It was the first peace agreement between Israel and an Arab country.

President Carter, President Sadat, and Prime Minister Begin clasp hands after signing the peace treaty in March 1979 at the White House

There was a change in the attitude of the USA after President Carter took office. In 1977, he expressed sympathy for a Palestinian homeland in the West Bank and the Gaza Strip. At the end of that year, President Sadat decided to seek peace with Israel. This was a momentous move and he became the first Arab leader to visit Israel when he spoke to the Knesset (Israeli parliament). Sadat's visit was returned by Prime Minister Begin some weeks later.

An American cartoon showing Jimmy Carter as Moses on top of the mountain with his Tablets of Stone

Jimmy Carter

▼ Born 1924, USA
▼ Military career – US Navy
▼ Successful peanut farmer
▼ President of the USA, 1976–1981
▼ Brought about Camp David Accord, 1978

Carter's greatest triumph in foreign affairs came in 1978, when he worked out the framework for the peace treaty between Egypt and Israel, known as Camp David. It was signed in 1979. President Sadat of Egypt paid tribute to Carter by insisting on only one signing of the Treaty in Washington, USA, saying, 'Jimmy Carter has done it and the show is his show.'

In November 1979, Islamic militants in Iran captured the United States' Embassy in Tehran and took a group of American citizens hostage. Carter took a strong position, refusing to meet their demands, and ordered a rescue attempt which was unsuccessful and had to be cancelled.

Although Carter's popularity declined sharply during his term as President, he successfully campaigned for re-nomination in 1980. In the election, however, Carter was overwhelmingly defeated by the Republican candidate, Ronald Reagan.

Menachem Begin, the Israeli statesman and leader

▼ Born 1913
▼ Trained as a lawyer at the University of Warsaw, Poland
▼ Fled to Lithuania in 1939 and fought against the Germans
▼ Israeli Prime Minister 1977–1983 First Israeli leader to sign a peace agreement with an Arab country in 1978
▼ Died in 1992

Menachem Begin has one of the most colourful histories of any Israeli leader. He fled from Poland in 1939 when the Germans invaded, and fought for a 'Free Polish' unit in the Soviet Red Army. Somehow Begin made his way to Palestine, where he was living by

1942. His military experience became invaluable to the Jews. Begin soon became a commander of the Irgun guerrilla group. They used terrorism to remove the British from Palestine, and Begin became a wanted man. Begin led the Irgun attack on the Palestinian Arab village of Deir Yassin in 1948. Once Israel became independent, Begin changed Irgun into the Herut political party. He became Prime Minister in 1977. In 1978 he and the Egyptian President, Anwar Sadat, were awarded the Nobel Peace Prize when they signed the Camp David Peace Accord.

In 1982 Begin ordered the Israeli invasion of Lebanon in order to clear the PLO from southern Lebanon. Criticism following the invasion led to Begin's resignation in 1983. He died in 1992.

Menachem Begin (top left picture) as a wanted terrorist on a British reward poster published in Palestine in the 1940s

A British cartoon from November 1977, showing Sadat walking from Egypt to Israel. Sadat was the first Arab leader to visit Israel. How does the cartoonist show that this was a dangerous move by Sadat?

Anwar Sadat

▼ Born 1918, Egypt
▼ Son of a hospital clerk
▼ Military career – Egyptian army
▼ President of Egypt, 1970–1981
▼ Signed Camp David Peace Accord, 1978
▼ Assassinated 1981

Sadat took part in the overthrow of King Farouk in 1952. He was elected President of Egypt in 1970. Following its defeat by Israel in the Six Day War of 1967, Sadat built up the military strength of Egypt, and, in 1973, launched the Yom Kippur War.

Partial success in this war gave Sadat a position of strength from which to talk to the Israelis. In 1977 he visited Jerusalem. He offered to recognise Israel and this move led to a peace treaty with them, and the withdrawal of Israeli soldiers from Sinai.

Sadat became hated by extremists who believed he had betrayed the Palestinians. In 1981 he was assassinated in Cairo by extremists from within his own army.

The Camp David Accords were bitterly opposed by some of the other Arab countries, such as Libya, Syria, Iraq, and Algeria. They attempted to disrupt Sadat's efforts to bring about peace between Israel and the Arab world. However, moderate Arab states, such as Jordan and Saudi Arabia, refused either to condemn or support Sadat.

Although Israel and Egypt could now exist side by side, the two leaders had to face much internal opposition over Camp David. The Israeli army had to evict Jewish settlers in Sinai; and right-wing Israelis were opposed to any surrender of what they believed to be Israeli territory. Two years after the peace treaty was signed, Sadat was assassinated by Arab extremists in Egypt.

A cartoon from the Saudi Arabian newspaper *Al-Riyadh* in 1980

A PLO anti-aircraft gun in Beirut in 1983

Israel still faced problems on its northern borders. The Palestine Liberation Organisation had concentrated its forces in the southern part of Lebanon and from there carried out terrorist activities against Israel. Following repeated attacks on villages in northern Israel, and the use of a suicide squad to kill 37 bus passengers, Israel decided to drive out the PLO forces from Lebanon. The first Israeli invasion of Lebanon began in 1978 but its forces were unsuccessful in removing the PLO and the United Nations sent troops to secure peace on the Israel-Lebanon border.

The activities of the PLO did not stop and Israel acted again when the PLO attempted to assassinate the Israeli Ambassador in London. Israeli forces invaded Lebanon in June 1982 and their aim was to destroy the PLO camps which had been shelling settlements in the north

of the country. The codename for the operation was 'Peace for Galilee'. Though the military objective was soon achieved, the Israeli forces continued to move further north into Lebanon – they were determined to crush the PLO once and for all.

The Israeli tactics meant that Syrian aircraft were shot down and civilians in Lebanon were bombed and killed. The major cities of Tyre and Sidon were left in ruins and the Lebanese capital, Beirut, was besieged. For ten weeks the Israelis shelled Beirut killing not only members of the PLO but also ordinary citizens. The world watched the devastation on television every day as thousands of Palestinian and Lebanese civilians were killed. Sympathy for Israel began to diminish. Eventually a ceasefire was made and an international force (American, French, and Italian troops) took the PLO survivors to surrounding countries. The PLO made its new headquarters in Tunisia.

The Israeli invasion of Lebanon in 1982

Operation Peace for Galilee, June 1982. Causes: PLO terrorists, having installed military bases in southern Lebanon, launch heavy artillery and rocket attacks against Israel.
Response: Israel enters Lebanon to destroy PLO bases along Israel's northern borders.

From an official Israeli booklet.

The heavy bombardments, the enormous destruction, and the high number of casualties among the refugees and the Lebanese population, were supposed to make it easier for the Israeli Army to occupy the area with a low number of casualties.
  An immoral act was done!
  Our government was prepared to cause heavy casualties on the other side, including civilians who are not party to the war between Israel and the Palestinians.

Professor Porath writing in an Israeli newspaper in June 1982.

1   Read Sources A and B. In what ways do these sources give you different interpretations about Operation Peace for Galilee?
2   How would you account for these differences?

The Arab-Israeli conflict and Lebanon

You have already seen why Israel invaded Lebanon in 1978 and 1982, but it is interesting to see how the conflict between the Palestinian Arabs and the Israelis almost destroyed a neighbouring country.

Lebanon was made up of three religious groups – Maronite Christians, Sunni Muslims and Shi'ite Muslims. Each shared in the running of the country, but there was always tension between the communities. After the PLO was forced out of Jordan (see page 45), new headquarters were set up in Beirut. By 1975, there were many thousands of PLO supporters living in the Palestinian refugee camps of Lebanon. From there they raided Israel. When Lebanon experienced Israeli reprisal raids on the refugee camps, tension between the groups grew, because the Christians opposed the PLO and attacked their bases. The Muslim groups supported the PLO and soon there was a civil war – Christians versus Muslims.

The situation became confused and chaotic when Syria entered the war, first on the side of the Muslims and PLO, and then on the side of the Christians. Eventually the Christian groups fell out with the Syrians and Lebanon moved into a state of anarchy. The two invasions by Israel added to the destruction of the country and Lebanon found itself occupied by UN forces and then an international force of British, French, Italian, and American soldiers. These forces were unable to keep the peace, and, following a suicide attack on the US military headquarters in October 1983, the international force pulled out. By the mid 1980s, the Israelis had pulled their forces back towards their border and created a buffer zone between Israel and Lebanon.

The effects of a car bomb in Beirut in 1986, during the Lebanese civil war

 UN forces in Lebanon in 1978

Though the PLO had been forced out of
Lebanon after Israel's invasion in 1982, the
Palestinians left in the refugee camps found
themselves being attacked by groups of Shi'ite
Muslims. The Shi'ites blamed the Palestinians for
the Israeli invasions and the subsequent troubles
of Lebanon. There were several massacres by
Shi'ites, the worst being at the Bourj-al Barajneh
camp in May 1985.

Though the civil war is now over, Lebanon is
still occupied by Israeli and Syrian forces, and
has thousands of Palestinian refugees within its
borders.

A roadside picture in southern Beirut in 1994,
showing the Ayatollah Khomaini. The Ayatollah
was the Shi'ite Muslim leader of Iran until his
death in 1989. His fundamentalist Islamic
views greatly influenced the ideas of Hamas
and Hezbollah (see pages 49 and 71).

Moves towards the Peace Accord

Following the Gulf War against Saddam Hussein in 1990, a conference was held in Madrid where US President Bush stated that any settlement in the Middle East would be based on the United Nations Security Council Resolutions 242 and 338 (see pages 34 and 39). Negotiations began after Madrid, but the PLO was not allowed to take any part, though a Palestinian delegation from the occupied territories was permitted after approval by the Israelis.

At the height of the Intifada (see page 47), there was a series of fourteen secret meetings between the PLO and Israeli government advisers held in hotels and country houses in Oslo, Norway. These meetings went on from January to August 1993 and were sponsored by Norway's Foreign Affairs Minister, Johan Jorgen Holst. In August the Declaration of Principles was agreed upon. The Declaration was an agenda for negotiations covering a five year interim period which would then lead to a permanent agreement based on Resolutions 242 and 338.

The main provisions were:
i Within two months of the Declaration coming into force, the Israeli forces would begin to withdraw from the Gaza Strip and Jericho (a town on the West Bank). The Israeli forces would be replaced by a Palestinian police force.
ii Israel would retain control of external relations and foreign affairs.
iii Once the Israeli withdrawal was complete, the Israeli government would transfer to authorised Palestinians civil power over education and culture, health, social welfare, direct taxation, and tourism.
iv Within nine months of the withdrawal, Palestinians in the West Bank and Gaza would hold elections for a Palestinian council which would be responsible for these areas of control, plus others to be negotiated, but not defence or foreign affairs.
v No later than two years after this, Israel and the Palestinians would start negotiations on a permanent agreement and address such issues as Jerusalem, settlements and the 1948 refugees.

The negotiators at Oslo, January-August 1993. This photograph of the participants was only released in January 1994, on the death of Johan Jorgen Holst (seated centre).

The history of the Arab-Israeli conflict has always been an international one. It has never been simply a local problem. Foreign powers have been involved since 1914, and, since 1973, the whole world has been affected by the rise in oil prices which are a consequence of the Yom Kippur War.

Britain's involvement in the problem

To gain help during the First World War, Britain made promises about a homeland to both the Arabs and the Jews.

At first Britain saw the area as being very important because of its position near the Suez Canal and on the Mediterranean Sea. For this reason, Britain wanted to be involved in Palestine. Yet, when the situation in Palestine became very difficult for Britain, the Government pulled out quickly.

In 1956 Britain interfered in the Middle East to try to protect its interests in Suez. This may have increased the tension and worsened relations between Israel and its Arab neighbours.

What effect did Britain have on the Arab-Israeli conflict? How did the involvement of Britain change the situation?

Try to do the same for the following countries and groups, and think how their involvement affected the conflict between Arabs and Jews. You will have to review a lot of the things which you have read and learnt already.

a The USA. Did it do too much to back up Israel, especially during the Cold War period?

b The USSR. Did they get too close to Nasser and other Arab rulers?

c The United Nations Organisation. Did it do enough to keep the peace at crucial times? (Read pages 65-67)

d The Arab states. Did they do enough to support the Palestinians?

The changing British attitude towards Palestine

1920
'Palestine will make a good base for our soldiers. We must stay here and try to keep it.'

1948
'Things are getting far too difficult here. It's no longer safe, lets go.'

Interpretations of history: The work of the United Nations Organisation

The UN has been involved in the Arab-Israeli conflict since 1947. It produced the Partition Plan and an armistice in the 1940s; and intervened in 1956 to stop the fighting, sending a number of peace keeping forces into the area. In addition, the UN has given aid to the refugees in the camps. Has the UN done enough in the Middle East? First study the evidence here before coming to your own conclusion. Also look at the information on pages 20, 22–23, 32–3, 34, 39, 42–3, and 61.

Help for the refugees

A
A UN truck delivers supplies to an Arab refugee camp

B

This refugee problem has been artificially maintained for political motives. Recent years have seen great expansion of Middle East economies, but the Arab governments have so far stopped the refugees from sharing this. The vast Arab words could find homes for a million refugees.

Abba Eban, Israeli Ambassador to the UN, 1958.

'The foreign press come here and take pictures of us standing in queues to get food rations. This is no life.'

'For twenty-two years we waited for the United Nations, for liberty, for freedom and democracy. There was no result.'

'We continued to refuse houses and compensation offered by the UN to settle us in our host countries. We wanted nothing short of our return to our homeland.'

Extracts from Palestinians commenting on the work of the UN.

1 What evidence can you find in Sources A, B and C to support the view that the UN has not done enough in the Arab-Israeli conflict?

The intervention of the UN in 1956

Following the invasion of Egypt by Israel, and the bombing of Egyptian airfields by Britain and France in 1956, the UN issued Resolution 997 to try to stop the fighting.

The General Assembly
Noting the disregard of the Arab-Israeli Armistice (1949) on many occasions by those who signed it; and that the armed forces of Israel have moved deeply into Egyptian territory in violation of the Armistice of 1949;
Noting that armed forces of France and the United Kingdom are conducting military operations against Egypt;

Noting that traffic through the Suez Canal is now interrupted to the serious disadvantage of many nations;
Expressing its grave concern over these developments;
Urges as a matter of priority that all those now involved in hostilities in the area agree to an immediate ceasefire and stop the movement of military forces into the area;
Decides to stay in emergency session until this resolution has been acted upon.

From UN Resolution 997 (ES-I) passed at an emergency meeting of the UN on 2 November, 1956. [Three days later British and French soldiers invaded the Suez Canal area.]

2   What evidence is there in Source D to support the view that the UN was not effective?

Peace keeping

A cartoon from the British newspaper *The Daily Express* 23 November 1956. The figure in the middle represents the UN, 'Dag's UNO police' refers to the UN Secretary-General, Dag Hammmarskjold. The figure on the left is meant to be Nasser, and the one on the right is Britain. The original caption said, 'Er – are you guarding me – or am I guarding you?'

"OBSERVED ANY TRUCE YET?"

F A cartoon which was printed in the British newspaper *The Sun* in July 1967 following the Six Day War

In May 1997 the United Nations Organisation criticised the Israeli security forces for using torture to obtain statements from prisoners. Some think this was too little and too late, Palestinian supporters and independent organisations had been criticising this practice for some time.

 G

Israel is not the only country where torture is carried out. We know of at least 90, but they all try to hide it. If Israel becomes the first state in today's world to openly and officially legalize torture, it would be a grave setback to human rights in the entire world.

Pierre Sane, Secretary-General of Amnesty International, 1996.

3 What evidence can you find in Sources E and F to support the view that the UN was not effective in the Arab-Israeli conflict?

4 'The UN did all it could to ease conflict in the Middle East.' Do you agree with this interpretation of the UN? Use the evidence in this feature and what you have learned from the rest of the book to explain your answer.

The role of women in the Arab-Israeli conflict

One of the most interesting features of the Arab-Israeli conflict has been the part played by women. Women on both sides of the conflict have played an important role in peace and war, for example Golda Meir (Prime Minister of Israel 1969–1974), Hanan Ashrawi (leading Palestinian peace negotiator), and Leila Khalid (a Palestinian terrorist in the 1970s). This feature examines in closer detail the varied contribution of women to the Arab-Israeli conflict.

 A

 B

A female fighter in the Jewish Haganah, 1948

Leila Khaled, a PLO guerrilla photographed in 1970

Women have risen to the top positions in both Israeli and Arab organisations. In 1969 Golda Meir became the Prime Minister of Israel and one of the world's first female premiers, (you can read more about her in the biography on page 39). Source C shows PLO leader Yasser Arafat with Hanan Ashrawi, one of his closer advisers and a leading member of the PLO.

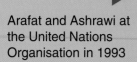 C

Arafat and Ashrawi at the United Nations Organisation in 1993

What have women said about the conflict?

 D

Women's participation in the struggle of the Palestinians for their homeland can be divided into three stages.

In the first stage (1882–1948) the participation of women was largely passive, inarticulate and unorganised. In 1921, Palestinian women took their first step towards organised activities by setting up The Arab Women's Society, which played an important part in organising demonstrations against Zionists. In 1948 one woman, Helwa Zaidan, is known to have picked up her son's weapons after he and his father were killed before her eyes, and to have fought until she too was killed.

The second stage (1948–1967) is characterised by a retreat from direct struggle. During this time social, charitable and only surface level political activity are dominant.

The third stage (1967–1987) saw women become more active. They took part in the planning and carrying out of armed operations. Leila Khaled is perhaps the best known among them. Many women were sent to prison for anti-occupation activities. It became the movement's policy to recruit women. Women had always contributed to the national cause in all struggles. They became visibly involved in the movement and received military training.

Hamid Kazi, an Indian feminist writer, writing about Palestinian Arab women and their role in the resistance. This was written in 1987.

 E

I had no idea what the women's prison was like, and my thoughts were wandering as I sat in the jeep, handcuffed and blindfolded and surrounded by police. Are the women allowed books? Visitors? Even though I knew the transfer to Rameleh meant I was going to get a longer imprisonment than I had expected, I was looking forward to meeting all the women I had heard so much about over the years – heroines, freedom fighters, strong women who had given up everything for the cause...

I turned my face and a sharp woman's voice ordered me: 'keep your face to the wall, Arab bitch, and don't move.'

All along the corridor of cells I heard: 'Be brave, sister.' Voices, faces, trying to console me. 'Be strong, comrade, don't worry. Don't let them frighten you,' the bruised faces were saying, smiling at me from behind the bars...

My brother's face came to my mind, thin and pale, the way he looked when I visited him in prison. 'Prison is a school', he used to say.

After two hours of study we would all go to the yard for physical training. We all loved that part of the day, running and jumping – it was vital that we kept fit. After dinner we would start our political education sessions. As these were not allowed, we had to post guards to keep watch.

Laila al-Hamdani was arrested and put in an Israeli prison for three years for her political activities. These are some of her memoirs.

 F

The Israeli woman is a natural part of the family of Jewish people and the female makes up a practical symbol of that. But she is a wife and a mother in Israel, and therefore it is of her nature to be a soldier, a wife of a soldier, a sister of a soldier, a grandmother of a soldier. This is her reserve service. She is constantly in military service.

Geula Cohen, Israeli MP and former member of the Stern Gang, writing about the Israeli woman, 1978.

1   After studying all of the sources in this feature (and page 39), do you think there has been any difference in the part played by Arab and Jewish women in the Arab-Israeli conflict? Explain your answer.
2   Why do you think the part played by women is less well known than that played by men?

6 Towards the present day situation

Shimon Peres and Yasser Arafat in Stockholm, 1996

In early September 1993, shortly before the Oslo Agreements (see page 63), Yasser Arafat and Prime Minister Rabin made mutual concessions. Israel recognised the PLO as 'the representative of the Palestinian people and would commence negotiations with the PLO within the Middle East [peace] process.' The PLO agreed to 'renounce the use of terrorism' and promised to 'discipline any member of the PLO who violated the Agreement'. These commitments were quite astonishing and there were mass rallies and street parties in the West Bank and Gaza where the Palestinian flag could now be flown legally.

However, there were some members of the PLO who remained unconvinced by Oslo. It was said that too much had been surrendered to Israel; and members of the extreme groups – Popular Front for the Liberation of Palestine, and the Democratic Front for the Liberation of Palestine – said that they would work against the 'Agreement of shame'.

The negotiations on the Oslo Declaration began in October 1993 and there were immediate disagreements about the area of land around Jericho which the Palestinians would control. Israel specified 24 square kilometres and Arafat demanded 350 square kilometres. The first agreements after Oslo were signed at Cairo on 9 February 1994. It became clear that Israel had scored a major victory here – Jericho was not to grow beyond the confines specified by Israel and the Jewish settlements in Gaza would remain under Israeli control at all times. Rabin won more applause in 1994, when a treaty was signed with King Hussein of Jordan. Israel's eastern border now seemed secure following Hussein's decision to give up all claims to the West Bank in 1988.

However, there were many Israelis who opposed the new peace agreements. One such person was Baruch Goldstein, a major in the Israeli army. On 25 February 1994, he shot dead 29 Palestinians at prayer in the Al-Ibrahimi Mosque, Hebron. This massacre immediately sparked off riots in Gaza, Jerusalem, Nablus, Ramallah, and Hebron. 33 Palestinians were killed in the disturbances and Rabin once again sealed off the West Bank and the Gaza Strip. A curfew was placed on the citizens of Hebron – 120,000 Palestinians were punished to guarantee the safety of 450 Jewish settlers in the area.

Hamas retaliated by killing Israeli security officers, and, in April, a car bomb killed 8 Israelis and wounded 40. Hamas were sending a signal to Israel, that even if the PLO and Arafat's followers did nothing, then it was not safe to assume that all Palestinians would remain silent and inactive.

Hamas then indicated to Israel that they would cease their activities if Israel:

i   withdrew to their 1967 borders
ii released all Palestinian prisoners
iii permitted elections to a sovereign body that would represent all Palestinians.

Hamas and Hezbollah (a fundamentalist Islamic group) have continued to struggle against Israel and have used suicide bombers on several occasions. Israel has responded in its customary way – swift retaliatory attacks. Leaders of Hamas have been murdered by Israeli agents and helicopter gunships attacked Hezbollah bases in Lebanon in early 1996.

The Middle East Peace Accord was signed by Yasser Arafat of the PLO and Prime Minister Yitzhak Rabin of Israel in a ceremony at the White House on 28 September 1995. The historic handshake between the two men seemed to signal an end to the problems of the Middle East.

However, killings inside Israel and the occupied territories did not stop after the Peace Accord. Since Oslo, more than 300 Palestinians and 150 Israelis have been killed. In November 1995, Prime Minister Rabin was assassinated at a peace rally by an Israeli student, Yigal Amir, who was strongly opposed to the surrender of any land to the Palestinians.

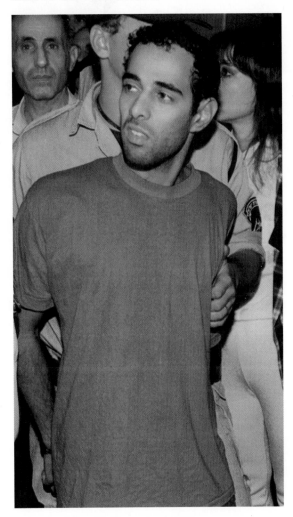

Yigal Amir, who assassinated Yitzhak Rabin in November 1995

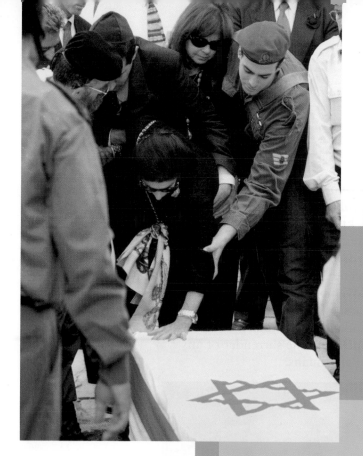

The funeral of Yitzhak Rabin

Yitzhak Rabin

▼ Born 1922
▼ Fought with the Palmach against the British until 1947
▼ Became Chief of Staff of the Israeli army in 1964
▼ Ambassador to the USA, 1968–1973
▼ Prime Minister 1974, and 1992–1995
▼ Assassinated 1995

Yitzhak Rabin was born in Jerusalem and fought to remove the British from Palestine. He was imprisoned by the British from 1946 to 1947. Rabin followed a military career until 1967 when, after the Six Day War, he retired from the army and became Ambassador to the USA. He entered the Knesset in 1974, and was Defence Minister from 1984 to 1990. Rabin became leader of the Labour Party in 1990 and Prime Minister in 1992. In 1995 he agreed to the signing of a Peace Accord with the PLO leader Yasser Arafat, which gave the Palestinians home rule in Gaza and Jericho. Opposition to this Peace Accord resulted in Rabin's assassination in 1995 by a Jewish Nationalist.

In the elections which followed Rabin's death, Israel chose a new leader – Benjamin Netanyahu. Netanyahu was elected on a tough manifesto. He promised:

i   never to give up the Golan Heights
ii to stick by the Oslo Agreements, but to build more Jewish settlements on the West Bank
iii that he would take part in talks on the status of the West Bank, but would not discuss Jerusalem.

However, Netanyahu only just won the Israeli election. He won 50.4% of the votes cast – a very small majority. Since becoming Prime Minister, Netanyahu has kept some of his promises. The ban on Jewish settlements on the West Bank has been ended, and bulldozers have been used to clear Arab houses in East Jerusalem and other sites on the West Bank. Land confiscation has continued, and the construction of a network of settler roads has begun. These roads in the West Bank and Gaza will be off limits for Palestinians.

▲ Armed Israeli police stop and question a Palestinian Arab in Hebron on the West Bank in January 1997

An Israeli bulldozer prepares to flatten an Arab house on the West Bank in February 1997, to make room for a larger Israeli settlement there

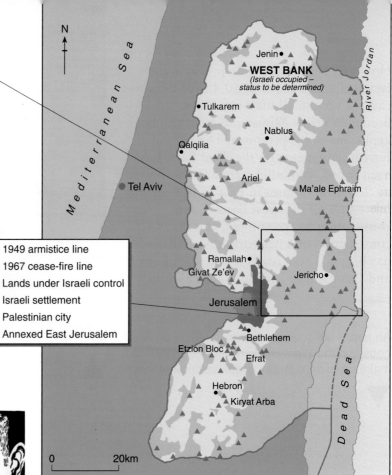

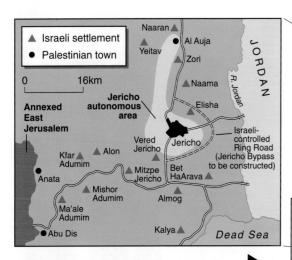

The Israeli occupied West Bank, showing the location of Jewish settlements and the autonomous area around Jericho which is now under direct Palestinian control

Map legend:
- ▲ Israeli settlement
- ● Palestinian town

0 — 16km

Annexed East Jerusalem

Jericho autonomous area

Israeli-controlled Ring Road (Jericho Bypass to be constructed)

- — 1949 armistice line
- --- 1967 cease-fire line
- Lands under Israeli control
- ▲ Israeli settlement
- ● Palestinian city
- Annexed East Jerusalem

NETANYAHU'S PATENT PEACE PROCESSOR

▲

A British cartoon from 1996. The Dove of Peace is inside a food processor. The blades are in the shape of the Israeli Star of David. Will Netanyahu press the button that destroys peace?

▼ Military career – took part in Israeli commando raid on Beirut airport, 1968
▼ His brother was the only Israeli killed during the Entebbe raid
▼ Israeli delegate to USA
▼ Became leader of the right wing Likud Party, and Prime Minister

Netanyahu became known outside Israel as the spokesman for the Israeli government during the Gulf War. He was seen as being articulate, younger, and more 'western' than most Israeli politicians. He became leader of

Benjamin Netanyahu

Israel in 1996 following the assassination of Yitzhak Rabin. 'Bibi' as he became known, was the champion of those right wing Israeli nationalists who did not want to give concessions to the Palestinians. His decisions to open up the tunnel under Old Jerusalem in 1996; to end the ban on Jewish settlements in the West Bank; and to send bulldozers to clear Arab houses in East Jerusalem in 1997, each sparked protest and violence. Netanyahu's willingness to risk the peace process brought about some distrust from world opinion.

In 1997 Netanyahu's position was brought into question when he was accused of corruption in the appointment of a senior government officer.

In spite of Netanyahu's hawkish moves, there are still many Jews who feel that the Palestinian Arabs have no right to be in Israel. This photograph shows an Israeli soldier, Noam Friedman (from the West Bank Jewish settlement of Ma'ale Adumim), who shot and wounded a number of Palestinians in Hebron on 1 January 1997. He is pictured being disarmed by a fellow soldier.

Benjamin Netanyahu and King Hussein of Jordan console the family of one of the 7 Israeli schoolgirls killed by a Jordanian soldier in March 1997 (also see page 4)

If you now return to page 4 and re-examine Sources A and B, you can see that you (or the conflict) has come full circle. Is there a solution?

The War and Peace rollercoaster

1947 United Nations partition plan

1949 Agreements for cease-fire and peace treaty signed

1956 United Nations force Britain, France, and Israel to withdraw from Suez

1967 United Nations calls for a cease-fire in the Six Day War

 A Jews are beaten and forced to flee their homes in anti-Jewish Pogroms in Kiev, 1881

B As Israeli soldiers attack, Arabs are forced to flee from their homes in the West Bank and attempt to cross the River Jordan, 1967

Change and continuity. (Sources A & B) No matter who started the fighting, it always seemed to be the ordinary people who suffered the most.

C Jews gather at the Wailing Wall Jerusalem, just after East Jerus. had been captured by the Israel. 1967

1948–1949 War

1967 War

1968 PLO and Israeli attacks or civil aircraft

1956 War

1979 Camp David peace treaty between Egypt and Israel

1993 Secret talks in Oslo between Israel and PLO

1995 Peace Accord signed between Israel and the PLO

Similarity and difference. (Sources C & D)
The Holy sites in Jerusalem are of great importance to both the Arab Muslims and the Jews.

E

Change and continuity. (Sources E & F)
The top photograph was taken in 1973. The bottom one shows the same two women in 1993. Twenty years on and these women are still able to say exactly the same things.

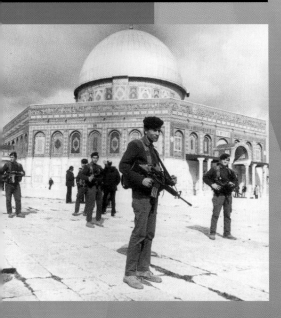

D

Soldiers of the Israeli army on guard outside the Dome of the Rock in Jerusalem, one of Islam's holiest sites. It was the opening of a tunnel under this building in 1996 which sparked off violent protests by the Arabs.

F

1995 Prime Minister Rabin of Israel was assassinated

1978 PLO suicide squad killed 37 Israelis

1982 Israel invaded Lebanon to drive out the PLO

72 PLO attack Israeli hletes at the unich Olympics

1973 War

1981 President Sadat of Egypt was assassinated

1997 Jordanian soldier murdered 7 Israeli school girls

*U*pdates

The peace process slowed down during 1997. Netanyahu continued to maintain his stance with regard to Jewish settlements on the West Bank, and to continued occupation of key places in that area.

Hamas continued its violent bombing campaign against Israel, and several civilians were killed in one attack on a Tel Aviv cafe. Such activity continues to play into the hands of the Israeli hard-liners.

1997 also saw fears about the future leadership of the PLO. There have been rumours about the failing health of Yasser Arafat, and it is thought that he could be replaced by a more hard line person. Netanyahu's own position has also not been secure, because of political scandals; and Israel's questionable stability could be rocked even further if there has to be another Israeli general election.

*U*pdates

*I*ndex